Seventy-Five Key Lessons in History

75 One-Page History Lessons Every
Student Should Know
with Intriguing History Games

By John De Gree

Classical Historian, Inc.

Table of Contents

Introduction_____6
I. Intriguing History Games_____7
II. Ancient and Medieval History
    1. The Fertile Crescent_____13
    2. Ancient Egypt_____16
    3. Mesopotamia_____18
    4. The Hebrews_____22
    5. Ancient Civilizations of Asia_____25
    6. Ancient Greece_____28
    7. Athens_____31
    8. The Roman Republic_____34
    9. The Roman Empire_____37
    10. Christianity_____40
    11. Important Leaders in the Ancient World_43
    12. The Age of Barbarians_____46
    13. The Romanization of Europe_____49
    14. Foundation of European Kingdoms_____52
    15. Medieval England and the Law_____55
    16. The Crusades_____58
    17. Aztecs, Incas, Maya_____61
    18. Homes of Native Americans_____64
    19. Technology_____67
    20. Medieval Warriors_____70
    21. Royal Power_____73
    22. Medieval Warfare_____76
    23. Four Interesting Medieval People_____79
    24. Famous Medieval Leaders_____82
    25. A Review of the Middle Ages_____85

III. Early and Modern World History
    26. The Renaissance_____89
    27. Beginning of the Renaissance_____91

28. The Renaissance in the South_____95
29. The Renaissance in the North_____98
30. The Age of Exploration_____101
31. The Reformation and Martin Luther____105
32. The Spread of the Reformation_____108
33. The Catholic Reformation_____110
34. The Rise of Empires_____114
35. The Commercial Revolution_____117
36. Ruling Houses of Europe _____120
37. Religious Wars and Kings' Wars _____123
38. Science, Inventions, and Medicine_____128
39. Philosophy, Astronomy, Mathematics and Physics_____131
40. The Age of Absolutism_____135
41. The Age of Revolution, 1776-1848_____140
42. The Industrial Revolution_____142
43. Peace, Free Trade, and Liberalism_____146
44. British Colonialism_____149
45. The Radical Left_____152
46. Nationalism and Unification_____156
47. World War I_____159
48. Totalitarianism_____162
49. World War II_____165
50. Rise and Fall of Communism_____168

IV. American History
51. The Discovery of America_____173
52. Native Americans_____176
53. Spanish Colonies in North America____179
54. French Colonies in North America_____183
55. The Founding of Jamestown, Part I____186
56. The Founding of Jamestown, Part II____190
57. Founding of Plymouth Plantation_____193
58. The First Thanksgiving_____196

59. The Mayflower Compact and The First Thanksgiving: Primary Sources_____198
60. The Southern Colonies_____201
61. The French and Indian War_____204
62. The Land Proclamation of 1763_____208
63. British Taxes and the Americans_____211
64. The Boston Massacre and the Boston Tea Party _____215
65. The Ideas of Revolution_____219
66. Lexington and Concord: April 19, 1775_223
67. Siege of Boston_____226
68. The Declaration of Independence _____229
69. Early Battles and the Winter at Valley Forge _____223
70. The French and Southern Phase of the War _____237
71. The Trans-Mississippian West, 1865-1890 _____240
72. America Enters the World Stage and World War I, 1898-1918_____245
73. The Roaring Twenties_____247
74. World War II_____250
75. The 1960s_____253

Introduction

Seventy-Five Key Lessons in History is designed to preview or review history in a time-efficient manner. Each succinct lesson contains key vocabulary words that are presented in bold and then defined on the next page. It is broken into three sections: Ancient and Medieval History, Modern World History, and American History. John De Gree is author of lessons 1-40 and 51-70. Dr. Mike Allen is author of lessons 41-50, 71-75, and edited lessons 51-70.

How is *Seventy-Five Key Lessons in History* useful?

>**1. Time-Efficient**: The teacher can take a lesson and teach it immediately. The teacher need not spend any time preparing for the lesson. The first four games in this book, The Word Game, History 20 Questions, Playing Games A. and B. with Multiple Lessons, and History Illustration, require no preparation. Read the lesson with your students, read out loud the vocabulary words, and play the game. We strongly recommend playing The Word Game with each new lesson. Depending on the size of your history class, each lesson could take one classroom hour.

>**2. Fun and Educational**: Learning history with games is fun, and many kids learn better when they can play a game with the materials. Learning history is valuable for many reasons. Young kids like to play games. *Seventy-Five Key Lessons in History* combines fun and education to provide guaranteed strategies that work to teach history.

I. Intriguing Activities to Aid in Learning and Memorizing History

A. The Word Game

1. Students have in front of them the "Items to Memorize" list with the definitions from one lesson. One person chooses one and describes it, not saying the actual item. Other students guess which one is being described.
2. After the initial round, the teacher writes only the terms on the board, and students are not allowed to look at the definitions. Students then play the Word Game.
3. In the third round, students reread the lesson, choosing items that are not listed on the "Items to Memorize" list. Then, students play the Word Game with the new list. Note: Each student keeps his Item List a secret. If nobody can say what term is being described, the reader "wins."

B. History 20 Questions

One student chooses an item either from the "Items to Memorize" list, or from his own Items that he created from the previous game (Play the Word Game, number 3.) The student does not tell the other students what the item is. The other students have to ask questions that can only be answered with "yes" or "no." The first 10 questions are not allowed to be "Item-Specific." This means that the first 10 questions have to be general. For example, "Is the item from the Hebrews?" If no student is able to guess within 20 questions, the reader "wins."

C. Playing Games A. and B. with Multiple Lessons

1. Once your group has learned more than one History One Sheet, you can play these games with multiple sheets. The more sheets you use, the more challenging the games will be.
2. If your group has multiple students, we strongly suggest you break the kids up into teams and have team contests with the Multiple Sheets.

D. History Illustration

1. Players form 2 or more teams of 2 – 5 players.
2. How To Play: Split the players into teams. Choose one or more lessons you want to play with. Write the vocabulary words that are *nouns* on separate cards, one vocabulary word per card. Place the cards face down in the middle of the teams. Choose one person from each team to be the first to illustrate. One of the players chosen to draw picks a card from the deck. The players chosen to draw from each team see the card and have 10 seconds to think of an idea. Somebody says, "Go!" and the chosen players draw their ideas. Teammates guess what is being drawn. The players drawing may not say any words, and may only nod yes or no.
3. To Win: The team that guesses what is on the card within the time allotted, before the other team, gets one point. Before playing, teams agree on how many points will decide a game.

*OPTION: History Illustration BASEBALL

In this game, one team draws, while the other watches. If the drawing team guesses the card within one minute, it scores a "run." Play continues until there is one out. Once there is one out, it's the other team's turn to draw (bat). Play as many innings as you have time for!

E. Chronology Game

1. How to Play: Choose the lesson or lesson you want to review. Write down vocabulary words that are names of people or events on cards – one person or one event per card. Order the cards in chronological order. Write the order down on a master list. Have the students study the cards in order. Then, mix up the cards. Challenge the student to line the cards up as fast as he can. Or, split the group into teams and have the teams line up the cards in chronological order. Time the students. For every mistake, add 10 seconds.

2. How to Win the Game: The child who lines the cards up the fastest wins. For each card that is out of place, add 30 seconds to the final score.

F. The Baton Game

1. Players form 2 teams. Teams can have up to 20 students per team.

2. Preparation To Play: Students learn a number of lessons. The teacher writes the vocabulary words on cards: one vocabulary word per card.

3. To Play: One representative from each team approaches the front of the room, or if playing outside, he comes to the front of the group of students. Each representative has a piece of paper rolled up into a baton. The teacher will then choose a card, and explain the card without saying the vocabulary word. The first student to hit his hand

with a baton answers first. If the answer is wrong, the other team gains a point, and the other team gets a chance to answer. Whoever answers correctly first wins a point for his team. After each turn, the next player from each team will take the baton and come to the front to play. Each player is allowed to have only one guess. If neither student knows the answer, the teacher says the answer.

4. After each round, the student with the baton chooses which student to next have the baton. To speed things up, the teacher can count down from 10 or 5 to 1, so that the students choose someone quickly.

5. To Win: The first team to score a certain number of points wins.

*Fun Modification: Instead of having the students just hit the baton when they know the

answer, they can turn around, jump up once, and then hit the baton. The movements can be modified in any way you choose.

G. History Charades

1. The teacher chooses which lesson or lessons to review, and writes the nouns on cards: each card with one noun.

2. Most likely, your students will have never played charades before, and you will have to teach them some basics of sign language. Tell students that Mimes are not allowed to say any words. The first thing the Mime does is show with his fingers how many words are in the answer. Once his team shouts out the correct number, the Mime nods yes and moves on. Through acting out what is on the card,

the teammates make guesses. If the Mime grabs his ear, this means, "Sounds like." The Mime will then act out something that sounds like the word that is on the card. This is done if the card is especially hard.

3. To Play: Students are broken into teams. The cards the teacher has explained are placed face down in a single deck. One person from one team begins the game by choosing the top card from the deck. Then, the teacher says, "Go," and the Mime has 60 seconds to act out what or who is on the card. Only the Mime's team is allowed to guess by shouting out loud. The other students are watching and thinking. If the team guesses correctly, the team earns 2 points. After the 60 seconds are up, if the Mime's team is unable to guess the card, the other teams then writes the answer down. The Mime then reads out loud the card, and whichever team has the correct answer receives a point. Then, the next team gets a chance.

4. To Win: The team with the most points wins.

H. Fencing for Cards – History and Action Game

1. Equipment Needed: Styrofoam Cups, Scotch Tape, and Noodles used in Pools as Floatation Devices. Note: The first part of this game is the same as the Baton Game.

2. Preparation To Play: Students learn a number of lessons. The teacher writes the vocabulary words on cards: one vocabulary word per card.

3. To Play: One representative from each team approaches the front of the room, or if playing

outside, he comes to the front of the group of students. Each representative has a piece of paper rolled up into a baton. The teacher will then choose a card, and explain the card without saying the vocabulary word. The first student to hit his hand with a baton answers first. If the answer is wrong, the other team gains a point, and the other team gets a chance to answer. Whoever answers correctly first wins a point for his team. After each turn, the next player from each team will take the baton and come to the front to play. Each player is allowed to have only one guess. If neither student knows the answer, the teacher says the answer.

4. Fencing: Then, each player tapes a Styrofoam cup on the hip opposite the strong arm of the participant, and with the strong arm, he holds a Noodle that is commonly used in a pool as a floatation device. For example, if a player is right-handed, then the Styrofoam cup is taped onto his shirt at the left waist. Use scotch tape, or another tape that is not too strong. To play, the player with the cup on his left side places his left hand behind his back. With the Noodle, the player then tries to hit the Styrofoam cup off of his opponent's shirt. Whoever knocks the cup off first wins one point for his team.

5. To Win: The first team that scores a certain number of points wins.

The movements can be modified in any way you choose.

2. Stage a battle with each team arming themselves with a Noodle and Styrofoam cup.

II. Ancient and Medieval History

1. The Fertile Crescent

The **Fertile Crescent** is an area in the Ancient Near East, including northern Africa, and encompasses the Euphrates, Tigris, and **Nile rivers**. Fertile means that crops grow well because the soil is rich. Crescent refers to the visible shape of the moon when it is less than half. Interestingly, the Fertile Crescent, in the shape of a crescent moon, is where the first great civilizations began. Thus, this area is the beginning of our story of American history, because the Fertile Crescent cultural lifestyle influences us today. America's cultural ancestors came from the Fertile Crescent.

The life of a hunter and gatherer is challenging. It is hard to build a permanent home, because when the animals move, a hunter must follow. These people were called **nomads**. Thus, hunters and gatherers never created large societies. This way of life changed in Sumeria, an early advanced Fertile Crescent civilization. Sumerians developed farming on a large scale. They learned that plants grow from seeds and how to grow crops. They also developed irrigation, a system to water large areas of land so crops could grow. Their food supply was stable, and the Sumerian population grew. With this stable food supply, Sumerians did not need to roam the land, and they built permanent shelters. They also created the first written language, called **cuneiform**, in about 3,000 B.C. The Sumerians wrote perhaps the oldest written story, *The Epic of Gilgamesh*.

Other great civilizations rose and fell in the Fertile Crescent. The Babylonians developed a **lunar calendar** with 12 months, a 7-day week, a 24-hour day, and a 60-

minute hour. King Hammurabi of Babylonia was the first to write down all laws and have them publicly displayed. **"Hammurabi's Code"** protected all people. Since the law was written and displayed, everyone knew what was the law and everyone had to follow it.

The Hittites were one of the first peoples to make iron. The Phoenicians were a sea-going people who traveled and traded throughout the Mediterranean Sea. Phoenicians created the world's **first alphabet.** Later, the Latins would alter this and create the Latin alphabet, which we use today. The Latins were the people who established the Roman Republic.

Some ancient people groups of the Fertile Crescent valued reading, writing, and arithmetic. People wrote on wet clay tablets that hardened. The Assyrians had a library in Nineveh with thousands of clay tablets containing arithmetic, literature, and chemistry. **The Chaldeans** were the first to divide the circle into 360 degrees.

In the Fertile Crescent, leaders, such as kings, chiefs and pharaohs, believed either that they were the representatives of God, or that they were one of the gods. Ideas of what was right and wrong depended solely on the leader. This meant that if the leader told a person to kill someone and the person followed through with this order, he did what was right. When the pharaoh of Egypt ordered someone killed, Egyptians took it to mean the voice of God and obeyed. Only one ancient people of the Fertile Crescent did not accept this view—**the Hebrews.** Hebrews believed in one God, the idea of monotheism.

Facts to Know for the Fertile Crescent

1. The Fertile Crescent: This is an area in the Middle East, also known as the Near East, in the shape of a crescent, that is the location of the first great civilizations.

2. Nomad: This is a person who does not have a permanent home but follows herds of animals.

3. Cuneiform: This is the written language of Sumeria and the world's first written language. It was not an alphabet but wedge-shaped characters.

4. Lunar Calendar: This calendar was based on the movement of the moon.

5. Hammurabi's Code: Hammurabi's Code was a publicly-displayed written set of laws of the Hittite Empire.

6. First alphabet: Phoenicians most likely created the first alphabet.

7. 360 degrees: Chaldeans divided the circle into 360 degrees.

8. Hebrews: The Hebrews were the first people who believed in one God.

9. Nile River: The Nile River is the largest river system in the world.

10. The Epic of Gilgamesh: This is perhaps the world's oldest story.

2. Ancient Egypt

Ancient Egypt was one of the first ancient civilizations to develop permanent homes, farming, and a very large and efficient government and society. Around 3100 B.C., **King Menes** united the communities of Upper Egypt and Lower Egypt to establish the first Egyptian dynasty. Egypt formed around the **Nile River**, one of the largest rivers in the world. It flows from south to north and empties into the **Mediterranean Sea**. It flows into the sea as many small rivers. Greeks believed the end of the river resembled the triangular fourth Greek letter, Delta, and so named the area the **Nile Delta**.

Religion played an important role in ancient Egypt. Egypt's leader, called **Pharaoh**, believed he would live eternally. After death, Egyptians embalmed the Pharaoh and wrapped his body in linen. Called a **mummy**, Egyptians then placed the dead Pharaoh in a tomb with many treasures that he could enjoy after death. Near the **Great Pyramid of Giza** stands a statue of one of Egypt's mythical creatures, the Sphinx. Called the Terrifying One, or the Father of the Dread, it is a statue of a lion's body and a human head. It stands on the bank of the Nile River, in Giza, Egypt, close enough to the Great Pyramids to be called their guardian. It is not exactly known when the Sphinx was built and which Egyptian built it, but historians believe it was constructed around 2,500 B.C. Some believe the **Sphinx** involved solar worship, but no one is completely sure.

The Pyramids of Giza, Egypt, were built around 2,500 B.C. as tombs for Pharaohs. The largest one, called the Great Pyramid of Giza, is the oldest of the three pyramids. Of the Seven Wonders of the Ancient World, it is the oldest and the only one that is still intact. Originally, the pyramids had a smooth outer surface. Egyptians believed that after death, their pharaohs entered into the after-life and could take material possessions and their slaves with them.

Most women in Egypt, just like most men, were poor farmers, servants, or slaves. But for those women who were free and upper class, they could own land and control property. The **Egyptian free woman** had complete equality of rights with men, could borrow money, sign contracts, initiate divorce, etc. The Egyptian woman was expected to run the household and be the primary caregiver to the children of the family. Common clothing for women was a dress worn low, near the ankles.

Ancient Egyptians were great warriors and conquered a large area of land. One of the vehicles Egyptians used in battle was the **war chariot**. It probably originated in Sumer, but Egyptians improved the chariot by making it lighter and faster. Nearly all parts of the war chariot were made of wood, including the tires and spokes. Chariots could not be used on rocky terrain because they would easily tip over. Egyptians fought with chariots in close ranks and used their bows to try to send a massive wave of arrows toward the enemy.

Facts to Know for the Ancient Egyptians

1. King Menes: Around 3100 B.C., Egyptian King Menes united Upper Egypt and Lower Egypt to establish the first Egyptian dynasty.
2. Nile River: The Nile River is the longest river in the world. Ancient Egypt developed around the Nile River.
3. Mediterranean Sea: The Nile River empties into the Mediterranean Sea. This sea is one of the most important in the ancient world.
4. Nile Delta: The Nile Delta is the lush farmland in the area where the Nile empties into the Mediterranean Sea. The Greeks named it this because it resembles the Greek letter Delta.
5. Pharaoh: The title of the leader of Ancient Egypt was Pharaoh.
6. Mummy: Ancient Egyptians embalmed and wrapped their dead pharaohs in linen. The dead pharaoh wrapped in lines is called a mummy.
7. Great Pyramid of Giza: The Great Pyramid of Giza is a large pyramid located near Cairo, Egypt, along with other large and smaller pyramids.
8. Sphinx: The Sphinx is an Egyptian mythical creature believed to protect the pharaohs and their families buried in the pyramids at Giza.
9. Egyptian Free Woman: A free woman of Egypt enjoyed more rights than many free women around the world in ancient times.
10. War Chariot: The Egyptians used the war chariot during battles.

3. Mesopotamia

Mesopotamia is often called the **"Cradle of Civilizations**." This means that many of the world's earliest civilizations started there. "**Mesopotamia**" means "the land between two rivers." It lies in Asia Minor, between **The Euphrates River and the Tigris River**. These two large rivers provided water for a fertile soil, drinking, and fresh water fishing. Today, the area corresponds to modern-day Iraq, Syria, and Kuwait.

In one of the earliest civilizations of Mesopotamia, writing developed called **cuneiform**. Cuneiform is the oldest known form of writing. Emerging around 3,000 B.C., it consists of wedge-shaped marks on clay tablets, made with a reed for a stylus. Cuneiform consists of pictures that represent words. Many civilizations used cuneiform, including the Sumerians, Akkadians, Eblaites, Elamites, Hittites, and others. The Phoenician invention of the **alphabet** replaced cuneiform. The alphabet used symbols to represent sounds and was easier to form words.

In Mesopotamian society, religion was very important. People believed in many gods, and that each civilization was protected by a god. **Ziggurats** were large structures of terraced step pyramids built for religious reasons by civilizations of Mesopotamia, such as Sumer, Babylonia and Assyria. It is not known exactly what ceremonies occurred on the ziggurats, but it is believed that on top of each ziggurat was a shrine and that it may have been the site of a sacred marriage during the new year festival. Historians think that Mesopotamians believed gods resided on top of the ziggurats.

The **Hanging Gardens of Babylon** in Mesopotamia was one of the Seven Wonders of the Ancient World. They were most likely built by **King Nebuchadnezzar II** of ancient Babylon around 600 B.C. There is no archaeological evidence of the gardens, but it is believed King Nebuchadnezzar II built them for his wife, Queen Amytis, who missed the green hills and valleys of her homeland. Some think that the gardens never existed except in Greek and Roman stories.

Facts to Know for Mesopotamia

1. Cradle of Civilizations: This term is used to describe Mesopotamia, because it is here where many civilizations began.

2. Mesopotamia: This means the land between two rivers.

3. The Euphrates River and the Tigris River: These two rivers form the boundary of Mesopotamia.

4. Cuneiform: Emerging around 3,000 B.C., this is the oldest form of writing and consists of pictures that represent words.

5. Alphabet: The Phoenicians invented the alphabet and consists of letters that represent sounds.

6. Ziggurats: These were large structures of terraced step pyramids built for religious reasons by civilizations of Mesopotamia

7. Hanging Gardens of Babylon: While there is no archaeological evidence for these, they were considered one of the Seven Wonders of the Ancient World.

8. King Nebuchadnezzar II: This king built the Hanging Gardens of Babylon for his Persian wife who missed the lush, green hills and valleys of her homeland.

4. The Hebrews

Western Civilization means the people that have certain shared ideas and beliefs. The idea of only one God, and that all people should be treated equally by the law, is part of **Western Civilization**. Many of these important ideas started with the Hebrews. The **Hebrews** were the world's first monotheists, which means they believed in only one God. Sometime between 2000 B.C. and 1600 B.C., the Hebrews believe that God spoke to one man, **Abraham**, and made a **covenant**, a special promise. God told Abraham that he would be the father of a great nation, the Hebrews. Abraham promised God that the Hebrews would be loyal to only Him. As long as the Hebrews were loyal, God told Abraham that He would protect the Hebrews. Abraham and his wife **Sarah** heard God and traveled from the land between the Tigris and Euphrates Rivers (Mesopotamia) all the way to Canaan, where the Hebrews later founded a country, called Israel. This is roughly in the area of the modern-day country of Israel. The Hebrews came to be called the Jews and their religion, Judaism.

The Hebrews believed one God was the Creator of all, and they believed in **morality**, the idea that there is a right and wrong. Hebrews taught that all people lived under God's dominion and were ruled by the same Truth. We can also call this a moral order. Sometime around 1300 B.C., God gave the Hebrews a set of laws to live by. Called the **Mosaic Law**, it is one of the first sets of written laws that deal with relationships (Hammurabi's Code does as well), placing importance on respecting parents and helping those in need. Have you ever heard of the Ten Commandments? They are part of the Mosaic Law.

Whereas other Fertile Crescent civilizations saw their rulers as either gods or representatives of God, the Hebrews saw their leaders as *servants* of God. This crucial difference between the Hebrews and other ancient civilizations has influenced great numbers of people over the last three millennia. As servants of God, Hebrews could not change the moral code established in Mosaic Law. Laws of Hebrew leaders could not be self-serving, but had to serve the God of the Mosaic Law. This idea, of a moral code established by God, which the rulers must live by and enforce, was passed onto all the cultures of Western Civilization, including the United States of America.

The government of the ancient Hebrews gives us an example of the first **balanced government** in the world. Balanced means that there was not one person ruling, but instead different people or groups held governmental powers. When power in government is separated, citizens have more liberty because no one person can take all the power and tell everyone else what to do. When the Hebrews conquered the Canaanites, beginning in **1407 B.C.,** the Hebrews were ruled by judges chosen from different tribes. From c. 1050 B.C. through 922 B.C., the Hebrews established the **Kingdom of Israel**. The kings did not hold ultimate power, but shared authority with prophets (messengers from God), the **Torah** (sacred scripture), and religious leaders.

Facts to Know for The Hebrews

1. Western Civilization: People that have shared beliefs, such as belief in one God and belief in morality as expressed in the Mosaic Law are part of Western Civilization.

2. Hebrews: The Hebrews were the world's first monotheists and established the Kingdom of Israel. Hebrews are the ancestors of modern-day Jews.

3. Abraham and Sarah: Hebrews believe God spoke to Abraham and Sarah are the first Hebrews.

4. morality: Morality is the idea that God established right and wrong for all people.

5. Mosaic Law: The Mosaic Law, including the Ten Commandments, is the law of the ancient Hebrews.

6. Balanced government: A balanced government is one in which power is separated and held by different people, making it difficult or impossible for one person to become a dictator.

7. Kingdom of Israel: From c. 1050 B.C. through 922 B.C., Hebrews established the Kingdom of Israel.

8. Torah: The Torah is the sacred scripture of the Hebrews.

9. Covenant: Covenant is the promise God made to Abraham. God promised Abraham many descendants and his protection, as long as the Hebrews remained faithful to God.

10. 1407 B.C: At approximately this date, Hebrews conquered the Canaanites.

5. Ancient Civilizations of Asia

Asia is the largest continent of the world and in ancient times it was home to many civilizations. It stretches from Arabia to the west to the shores of the Pacific Ocean in the east. In the north it lies above the Arctic Circle and in the south it has a tropical climate. It may be the most varied of continents in terms of climate and geography.

One influential ancient Asian was **Siddhartha Gautama**. He lived in India c. the 5th century B.C. He left his wife and child to search for what he believed to be enlightenment. He found that through meditation and giving up his desires and wants, he was able to achieve a type of peace that he could not otherwise. His followers say he became the "**Buddha**," meaning the "enlightened one." Millions of people today call themselves Buddhists. Buddhists strive to be peaceful by following the ways of Siddhartha Gautama. Buddhists do not say if there is a God or if there is not a God.

Beginning in the seventh century B.C., the Chinese built a wall of stone, brick, wood, packed earth, and other materials to separate itself from people to the north. The wall is actually a number of walls that are not connected, stretches east to west, and in the third century B.C., **Emperor Qin** (pronounced "Chin") expanded the wall. **The Great Wall of China** served not only defensive purposes, but also allowed China to impose taxes on imports and exports, and to control immigration. In the 1400s and 1500s, the Ming Dynasty strengthened and expanded the wall.

Confucius lived in ancient China in the 5th century B.C. He was a philosopher who lived during a time of violence. **Confucius taught** that individuals need to be respectful of their elders, their government, and all authority figures. He also taught that leaders need to be respectful of people under them, and that all people need to be patient. In ancient China, Confucius' thoughts received official approval and formed part of a national curriculum.

One of the most successful and ruthless Asian conquerors was **Attila the Hun**. Attila ruled the Huns and conquered immense territory in Asia and Central and Eastern Europe in the middle of the 5th century. Europeans called him the **"Scourge of God,"** which means the punisher. Huns were nomads who fought on horseback, shooting arrows and throwing javelins. Historians report that Attila's army completely destroyed cities, and after the destruction of the city **Naissus**, dead bodies clogged the Danube River for years.

Facts to Know for Ancient Civilizations of Asia

1. Asia: This is the largest continent in the world and has the most population.
2. Siddhartha Gautama: He lived in 5th century India and is the founder or inspiration of Buddhism.
3. Buddha: This means the enlightened one. Buddhists say that Siddhartha Gautama reached this stage, where he did not desire to possess anything and lived in peace.
4. The Great Wall of China: This is a series of defensive walls built in the north of China for protection.
5. Emperor Qin: Emperor Qin lived in the third century B.C. and greatly expanded building the Great Wall of China.
6. Confucius: He lived in the fifth century B.C. in China and was an influential philosopher.
7. Confucius' teachings: Confucius taught the importance of respecting your elders, authority, and tradition.
8. Attila the Hun: Attila was a fifth century Hun who conquered a large amount of land in Asia and in Europe.
9. Scourge of God: Europeans called Attila the Scourge (Punisher) of God, and believed that Attila was punishing the Europeans for not being good believers in God.
10. Naissus: Attila besieged and attacked this city of the Eastern Roman Empire. According to historians, dead bodies and bones littered the banks of a nearby river for years after the fighting.

6. Ancient Greece

Many argue the birthplace of **Western Civilization** is Ancient Greece. A seafaring people, living on rugged and mountainous terrain, the Greeks were pioneers in philosophy, drama, law, government, art, math, history, natural sciences, and more. Forming small political communities called **city-states**, ancient Greeks did not live in one country but many, smaller, independent societies. When challenged from abroad with conquest, Greeks banded together and fought. After over 1,000 years of freedom, ancient Greek city-states were eventually conquered by the Roman Republic

Religion played a crucial role in the life of ancient Greeks. Greeks worshipped many gods and had daily rituals honoring their deities. Today, we call the ancient Greek religion **Greek mythology.** In Ancient Greece, Greeks believed in many gods. **Zeus** was considered the king of the gods and men. He was the son of Rhea and Cronus. Greeks believed that Zeus, like other gods, interacted with humans, influenced human affairs and fathered many children with different women and goddesses. Symbols of Zeus are the thunderbolt, eagle, bull, and oak.

In the fifth century B.C., ancient Greeks built the **Parthenon**, a temple in Athens to honor the goddess Athena. Inside the Parthenon was a massive statue of Athena created of ivory and gold. The Parthenon is built in the **Classical style**, which refers to buildings of ancient Greece and ancient Rome. Columns and symmetry are two characteristics of Classical style.

Socrates, a 5th century B.C. Greek philosopher, is often called the "Father of Western Philosophy." We know about

Socrates mainly through the writings of **Plato**, one of his students. Socrates taught young men in the city of Athens during a time of war and is associated with the phrase "know thyself." He wanted his students to know the reasons for their actions and thoughts, and he questioned the belief in the gods of Athens. The city leaders convicted Socrates of corrupting the youth and he was forced to kill himself by drinking the poison **hemlock**.

Sparta was a city-state of Ancient Greece. Spartan men trained to be strong warriors from childhood and they were the best Greek warriors. From the age of 7, all boys left their mothers to live in barracks and train for war. Men could marry but could not live with their families until age 60. Slaves did most of the physical labor in Sparta. Sparta did not have a wall to protect the city because the warriors were so good that no enemy could break in. Women could run businesses and own property.

Facts to Know for Ancient Greece

1. Western Civilization: This refers to the customs and traditions that a number of countries in the world share, such as the idea of liberty, individual rights, and reason.
2. City-State: The city-state is a very small country. In Ancient Greece, societies were organized as city-states.
3. Greek Mythology: Ancient Greeks believed that various gods controlled nature and man. We call their religion "mythology."
4. Zeus: Greeks considered Zeus the king of gods and men. Symbols of Zeus are the thunderbolt, eagle, bull, and oak.
5. Parthenon: Greeks built this temple to honor the goddess Athena. It still stands today.
6. Classical Style: Classical style architecture refers to the style found in Ancient Greece and Ancient Rome.
7. Socrates: He was a Greek philosopher who is called the "Father of Western Philosophy."
8. Plato: Plato was a student of Socrates and wrote about what Socrates taught.
9. Hemlock: Hemlock is a poison Socrates was forced to drink that killed himself. The leaders of Athens did not like how Socrates made the young adults question authority and sentenced him to die.
10. Sparta: Sparta was a city-state of Ancient Greece and Spartan soldiers were perhaps the best warriors in the ancient world.

7. Athens

On hundreds of small islands and on steep mountains with rocky soil, groups of hearty men and women established the foundations of Western Civilization. For Western Civilization, the Greek city-state of Athens stands out because of all the cultural gifts this civilization passed on. In ancient Greece, there was no one nation of "Greece." Instead, there were a number of Greek cities, each with its own laws, customs, army, and its own way of living. Called **city-states**, these cities had various governments, ranging from the most democratic Athens to the militaristic Sparta.

During what historians call **Classical Greece** (c. 5th century to 3rd century B.C.), ancient Athenians chose the system of direct democracy. In direct democracy, citizens vote directly for all laws. At the same time in the Roman Republic, Romans practiced representative democracy. In representative democracy, citizens vote for representatives who make the laws.

Athens was the birthplace of both philosophy and democracy. **Philosophy** is the study of knowledge, truth, and the best way to live. **Democracy** is where each citizen votes on every law. **Socrates** (470-399 B.C.), the father of Western philosophy, taught Plato, who wrote that the goal in life was to pursue truth, goodness, and beauty. Athenians believed that citizens should be free, and that it was wrong to have an all-powerful king. Athenians had three branches of government—executive, legislative, judicial—with each branch having a separate job. They did this so no one Athenian would become too powerful.

In the fifth and fourth centuries B.C., Plato taught **Aristotle**, ancient Greece's most prolific writer on philosophy, government, and science. Aristotle believed that all people had a common human nature, that all people have reason, and that all should participate in government. He did not think there should be a certain group of special people in charge of government, but that all citizens over 18 should participate equally. (Some Athenian women were citizens but were not allowed to vote. Slaves, minors [those under 18], and foreigners living and working in Athens did not have citizenship rights.) Aristotle also wrote that the best life is lived by those who try to live lives of **virtue**. This means that if a person always tries to do the right thing, even when it is difficult or uncomfortable, he will live his life in the best way.

Aristotle wrote that there is something "just by nature." This means that justice cannot mean one thing in one society and another thing in another society, because there is a higher law than the one created by man. This idea can be called nature's law, or **natural law**. Aristotle also wrote that happiness is "activity of soul in accordance with nature," meaning a life lived in accordance with reason and virtue is a happy one.

The American Founding Fathers saw ancient Greeks and Romans as our ancestors and they even built many buildings in our nation's capital city to resemble those of ancient Greece and Rome. Our U.S. Capitol (where our Congressmen work), the Supreme Court building (where our most important judges work), and the White House were all built in the **Neoclassical architectural style** to resemble those found in ancient Greece and Rome.

Facts to Know for Athens

1. Athens: Athens was a city-state of Greece and is the birthplace of democracy.
2. City-state: This was a city that functioned as a country, with an army and government.
3. Classical Greece: Classical Greece refers to a specific time period, c. 5th century and into the 4th century B.C., when Athenians practiced democracy and achieved great cultural advancements.
4. Socrates: Socrates is known as the father of western philosophy.
5. Aristotle: Aristotle is perhaps Greece's most important thinker and most prolific writer on philosophy, government, and science.
6. Virtue: Virtue is behavior showing high moral values.
7. Natural Law: Natural law is the idea that something is just by nature for all and that this idea, Natural Law, comes from a source higher than man.
8. Neoclassical Architecture: This is an architectural style that resembles buildings of ancient Greece and Rome.
9. Philosophy: Philosophy is the study of knowledge, truth, and the best way to live.
10. Democracy: In democracy, every citizen votes for every law.

8. The Roman Republic

The Roman **Republic** (509 B.C. to 48 B.C.) was perhaps the world's greatest **representative government** in the ancient world. Romans tried to create a government in which its citizens were treated the same by the law, and where a strong man could not become the dictator. In the Roman Republic, citizens were adult, free males who lived within the Roman Republic and who were not from a colony or province. Before and after the Roman Republic, the world is full of examples of determined, brutal leaders who took over and ruled a government by force, yet in the Roman Republic, each citizen could vote, and the powers of government were separated into three branches.

All Romans had to follow the law. This idea is known as **"the rule of law."** It is important, because in most countries of the world then, and in many today, leaders do not have to follow the law and can change it as they like. In Rome, the laws, called the **Twelve Tables**, were publicly displayed, every citizen was under the law, and children memorized the laws. When laws are written, society is secure because everyone knows what is allowed or not allowed. The powerful cannot assert their will over others if it means breaking the legal code.

Romans also believed in freedom of thought, freedom of speech, that a person was **innocent until proven guilty**, and that the accused has a **right to confront his accuser**. All of these ideas are important in American society today. **Freedom of thought** means that each person has a right to think, even if his thoughts may offend others. **Freedom of speech** means that a person can say what he thinks, even if he opposes the government. When we say the accused has a right to confront his accuser and that a person is innocent until proven guilty, it means that a person accused of a crime has the right to see the person who accused him, and the accuser must present evidence to show guilt.

Cincinnatus was a 5th century Roman who wanted to farm his land. However, enemy tribes were attacking Rome and his fellow countrymen needed his military leadership. They made him dictator so that he could defend Rome, and give orders to everyone quickly and decisively. However, two weeks after the Romans defeated their enemies, Cincinnatus peacefully gave up his power and went back to being a farmer. Romans and historians honor Cincinnatus as an example of a great and humble leader. Many years later, after leading the Continental Army during the American Revolution, George Washington also stepped down from power, and he surrendered power again when he resigned after his second presidential term. Many historians say that Washington acted just like Cincinnatus, displaying courage in the same way.

Cicero (106 B.C. to 43 B.C.) was a Roman statesman who wrote about man and his rights. The American Founding Fathers read his works, which greatly influenced them. Cicero wrote that true law is based on reason and that it is the same for all men everywhere in the world. Like Aristotle, he wrote that all men everywhere are ruled by something called natural law that humans have because of their birth. No great person or leader gives this natural law to someone. We have it because we are born.

Facts to Know for The Roman Republic

1. Rule of Law: The "Rule of Law" is the idea that all people have to follow the law. In this way, leaders are limited and they cannot become dictators.
2. Innocent until proven guilty: This is the idea that the accused must prove that someone is guilty and that all people are assumed innocent before trial.
3. The right to confront the accuser: If someone accuses another of a crime, the accused gets to see who is accusing him and has an opportunity to defend himself in court.
4. Twelve Tables: These were laws of the Roman Republic, written and publicly-displayed in every major city.
5. Freedom of thought: This freedom is the right to think something, even if it offends another.
6. Representative government: This is a system where citizens vote for leaders and leaders make laws.
7. Cincinnatus: This Roman farmer assumed dictatorial powers to defeat an enemy of Rome then relinquished power to go back to farming.
8. Cicero: This Roman statesman believed in representative government and was killed because of his beliefs and writings.
9. Republic: A republic is a country with a representative government. Voters choose leaders and leaders make the laws.
10. Freedom of Speech: Freedom of speech means that a person can say what he thinks, even if these ideas are offensive or if the ideas oppose the government.

9. The Roman Empire

The **Roman Empire** lasted from 27 B.C. until A.D. 476. In many ways, it carried on the traditions and customs of the Roman Republic. Roman citizens enjoyed many rights and within the empire there was law and order, for the most part. However, in the empire, citizens were forced to worship the emperor as if he were a god. The old Roman religion was modified so that the emperor represented one of the many Roman **deities**, and the citizens were treated more as subjects than citizens. Slavery increased, and Rome expanded.

The Roman Empire began when the Roman Republic fell into **Civil War**, during the first century. For a variety of reasons, the Roman Republic experienced great challenges that caused the society to splinter into separate factions. Gaius **Julius Caesar** (100 B.C. – 44 B.C.) was a Roman general and statesman who seized power at the end of the Roman Republic. Caesar masterfully conquered the Gauls in present-day France, invaded Britain, and built the first bridge across the Rhine. The Roman Senate ordered Caesar to relinquish power, but when he crossed the **Rubicon River** he signaled to the Senate that he wanted to take over the government. The Senate then proclaimed him dictator. Senators resented Julius Caesar having so much power and killed him on March 15th, 44 B.C. More Civil War ensued until Octavian declared himself the first Roman Emperor and took the name **Caesar Augustus**. The Roman Empire existed until A.D. 476.

From the beginning of the Roman Republic (c. 5th century B.C.) to nearly the end of the Roman Empire (c. A.D. 476), the Roman soldier was perhaps the best-trained and most able soldier in the world. In the Republic, every Roman male had a duty to serve in the army. In the Empire, soldiers were professional. Historians call the first and second century the time of **"Pax Romana,"** which means Roman peace. During this time, inside the Roman Empire, the Roman soldiers enforced order and protected the people.

The **Pantheon** was a Roman temple built to honor all Roman gods. Emperor Hadrian completed the Pantheon in A.D. 126. The temple remains in excellent shape, in part because it was in use throughout the Middle Ages. In the seventh century, it was rededicated as the Christian church "St. Mary and the Martyrs." The building is an architectural wonder. The dome of the Pantheon weighs 4,535 metric tons. At the top of the dome is an opening, an oculus, that provides natural light and ventilation, and there is a drainage system to remove the rain. The Pantheon inspired many later architectural works.

Facts to Know for the Roman Empire

1. Roman Empire: This empire lasted from 27 B.C. to A.D. 476.

2. Deities: This word means gods.

3. Civil War: At the end of the Roman Republic, there was Civil War.

4. Julius Caesar: He was one of the most brilliant Roman generals and declared himself dictator at the end of the Roman Republic.

5. Rubicon River: This river marked an important boundary. If a Roman general marched his army over it going south, it meant he was taking his army to Rome and attempting to take over.

6. Caesar Augustus: He was the first Roman Empire and ruled from 27 B.C. to A.D. 14.

7. Pax Romana: Literally, this means "Peace of the Romans." During the first and second century of the Roman Empire there was relative peace and order in the empire.

8. Pantheon: Romans constructed this temple to all the gods. It is a magnificent building with a giant dome. It influences architecture today.

10. Christianity

During the first century, a new religion began that would eventually become the official religion of the Roman Empire and spread throughout the Western world. **Jesus Christ** was a Jewish carpenter born and raised in Roman-controlled Bethlehem and Nazareth in the ancient Near East. His followers, called **Christians**, taught that Jesus was the son of God, that he was a savior to all people, and that all people are called to turn from their selfish ways, ask God for forgiveness, and treat each other with love. Three centuries after the death of Christ, Christians compiled this message in the **Bible**, their holy book.

Christians believe that all people were created in the image of God, and that all people share the same nature. According to Christians, people know what is good or bad because God gave a **conscience** to all people. This law of nature exists outside of man's creation. Christians believed this idea over the centuries, and it found expression in the Declaration of Independence, when Thomas Jefferson wrote "all men are created equal" by their Creator.

The development of Christianity within the Roman Empire had ramifications not only for the empire, but for all of Western Civilization. The leader of the Roman Empire, the emperor, led the official Roman religion, which was **pagan**. The emperor took the title of **Pontifex Maximus**, meaning leader of the official pagan religion of Rome. This is known as the concept of **caesaropapism**. This was the idea that the leader of the government is the leader of the religion. When the **Roman Empire adopted Christianity** in A.D. 380, however, the emperors ceased being head of the religion. This fell to the bishop of Rome, who was called the **Pope**, forming a separation between the leader of the political world (the emperor) and the religious world (the Pope). Whereas the emperor formerly held ultimate authority in both the political and religious worlds, he was now limited by the Christian Church.

Governments in Western Civilization have expressed the understanding that the political world should be governed by someone different than the leader of the religious world. In North America, this idea can be seen in the constitutions of the English colonies, and in the United States Constitution, notably in the First Amendment. Americans may worship freely in any religion they choose, and they do not have to belong to a particular religious group. This concept of church and state having separate leaders had its beginnings with the Roman Empire. Nevertheless, governments of the east continued to be ruled by the idea of caesaropapism.

President Calvin Coolidge, on the 150th anniversary of the Declaration of Independence, wrote that the individual "is endowed with inalienable rights which no majority, however great, and no power of the Government, however broad, can ever be justified in violating. The principle of equality is recognized. It follows inevitably from belief in the brotherhood of man through the fatherhood of God." The belief that an **individual** has **rights** over the power of government is one of the great ideas of Western Civilization.

Facts to Know for Christianity

1. Jesus Christ: Jesus Christ is the founder of Christianity.
2. Christians: Christians are followers of Christ who believe Jesus was a savior to all people and that all people are called to turn from their selfish ways, ask God for forgiveness, and treat each other with love.
3. Bible: The Bible is the holy book of the Christians and was compiled three centuries after the death of Jesus.
4. Conscience: Christians believe that God gave all people a conscience, the faculty that allows humans to know what is good and bad.
5. Pagan: A pagan is someone who believes in many gods.
6. Pontifex Maximus: Pontifex Maximus is the title given to the leader of the Roman Church.
7. Caesaropapism: This was the idea that the leader of the government is the leader of the religion. Before the Roman Empire became Christian, the Roman emperor was the leader of the Roman Church.
8. A.D. 380: The Roman Empire adopted Christianity as the official religion.
9. Pope: The pope is the bishop of Rome, and after The Roman Empire adopted Christianity, the Pope became the leader of the Church in the Roman Empire.
10. Individual Rights: The idea that the individual has rights over the government is one of the great ideas of Western Civilization.

11. Important Leaders of the Ancient World

Augustus Caesar was the first Roman Emperor, ruling from 27 B.C. to A.D. 14. His rule marks the beginning of the Roman Empire. Born Gaius Julius Octavius, Romans gave him the name Augustus, meaning "The Revered One." Augustus was the great-nephew of Julius Caesar, and was both a ruthless and a skilled administrator. To seize power, Augustus ordered the murder of many of the Roman Republic's leaders, fought wars, and ordered the murder of Caesar and Cleopatra's alleged son. Augustus began two centuries of a Roman rule, called the "Pax Romana," that was relatively peaceful and very prosperous.

Cleopatra was the last pharaoh of Egypt and the last in the line of the Ptolemaic dynasty. After Alexander the Great conquered Egypt, the Macedonian Ptolemy family became the rulers of Egypt. Though a Macedonian, Cleopatra learned Egyptian and claimed she was the reincarnation of an Egyptian princess. Cleopatra most likely had a son with Julius Caesar. After Caesar's murder, Cleopatra aligned with **Marc Antony**. After Antony lost a battle against Augustus Caesar, Antony and Cleopatra committed suicide.

China gets its name from **Emperor Qin**, pronounced "Chin", who united and ruled China from 220-210 B.C. Emperor Qin greatly expanded the country and the Great Wall of China. He created a city-sized mausoleum guarded by the large Terracotta Army. The **Terracotta Army** was a huge group of life-sized figures made of unglazed clay. Emperor Qin was buried with the following terracotta figures: 8,000 soldiers, 130 chariots, and 670 horses, along with officials, acrobats, strongmen and musicians.

Pericles was a fifth century B.C. Greek statesmen who led Athens during one of its most accomplished periods in history. Called **Athens' Golden Age**, this time period witnessed great accomplishments in art, architecture, politics, and philosophy. The great Greek historian Thucydides called Pericles "the first citizen of Athens" because Pericles was so honored for his greatness. Pericles was a defender of democracy.

Facts to Know for Important Leaders of the Ancient World

1. Augustus Caesar: He was the first Roman Emperor, ruling from 27 B.C. to A.D. 14.

2. Cleopatra: She was the last pharaoh of Egypt and the last in the line of the Greek Ptolemaic dynasty.

3. Marc Antony: Marc Antony was a Roman general who allied himself with Cleopatra. Together, he and she lost a battle to Augustus Caesar. Cleopatra and Marc Antony committed suicide.

4. Emperor Qin: Pronounced "Chin," China gets its name from this leader. Emperor Qin expanded the Great Wall of China.

5. Terracotta Army: Emperor Qin built a massive army out of clay. It still exists today.

6. Pericles: He was a fifth century Greek statesman who defended democracy.

7. Athen's Golden Age: During the fifth century, Athens produced some of the world's most important literary, architectural, philosophical, and scientific creations.

12. The Age of Barbarians

The Age of Barbarians marks roughly the first 400 to 500 years of the medieval ages, from A.D. 476 to about 900 or 1000. Sometimes called "**The Dark Ages**," it was a time of violence, great uncertainty, and chaos throughout Europe and the former Western Roman Empire. As the Roman Empire crumbled, the **Germanic**, **Slavic**, and **Hun** peoples stepped in to take over. Although the **barbarian** tribesmen lacked the education, sophistication, and culture of the Romans, the barbarians eventually destroyed the Roman Empire and ruled Europe for centuries.

When Romans travelled into northern Europe, they came into contact with Germanic tribesmen, a people with a different culture and language than the Romans. One Roman author remarked that when he heard the Germanic peoples speaking, he could only hear the sounds of "bar bar bar bar." Because of this, Romans called people who spoke another language than Latin, as well as those who seemed uncultured, barbarians. The Germanic barbarians had no written language, a simpler political organization than the Romans, and worshipped trees and nature. Romans viewed many outside of its northern borders as barbarians, although they were diverse.

Other barbarians attacked the Roman Empire. From Asia came the **Huns**, warriors on horseback who invaded the peoples of Europe in the fifth century. **Attila** was chief of the Huns and one of the most feared conquerors in history. After laying waste to much of Italy and Rome in A.D. 452, Attila had plans to destroy the Vatican City in Rome. However, **Pope Leo the Great** rode out of Rome with his entourage and engaged Attila in discussion. No one knows what was said during this conversation, but Attila did not attack the Vatican City, leaving the early Christian Church intact.

Celtic and Slavic peoples also inhabited Europe. Like the Germanic tribes and Huns, they lacked a written language and were polytheists (believed in many gods). Celts were known as fierce warriors with a great sense of political equality. Celtic women could speak and vote in tribal councils and could carry weapons and fight in battle. Celtic peoples inhabited Central and Western Europe. Slavic peoples inhabited Central and Eastern Europe. It is believed Vikings (from Denmark, Norway, and Sweden) enslaved large numbers of Slavs, from which our English word "slave" originated.

The barbarians were **polytheists**; the Romans Christians. Some of the barbarians practiced human sacrifice; the Romans thought this practice horrifying. The barbarians lacked reading and writing; the Romans valued learning. In all societies, slavery was the norm. Contrary to popular belief, there is no evidence that Romans used toilet paper and barbarians did not. It appears that neither society used paper.

Throughout the old and crumbling Roman Empire, various barbarian tribes conquered and settled: the Angles, Saxons, and Jutes in Britain; the Franks and Burgundians in modern-day France; the Visigoths and Vandals in modern-day Spain and North Africa; the Ostrogoths in modern-day Italy; the Slavs in Central Europe; the Celts in modern-day Ireland, Scotland, and Wales. These peoples would eventually form the modern nations of Europe.

Facts to Know for The Age of Barbarians

1. Barbarians: Romans called the Germanic, Slavic, and Hun peoples barbarians because Romans couldn't understand their language and when these people spoke the Romans heard, "Bar bar bar."

2. Huns: Huns were Asians who attacked the Roman Empire.

3. Celts: Celts lived in Central and Western Europe during the Roman Empire.

4. Germanic Tribes: Germanic peoples lived throughout Europe and attacked the Roman Empire.

5. Slavs: Slavs lived in Eastern Europe during the Roman Empire.

6. Political Equality: This is the idea that all citizens have the same rights.

7. Attila the Hun: Attila was a very successful conqueror of the 5th century.

8. Pope Leo the Great: In A.D. 452, Pope Leo the Great persuaded Attila to not attack the Vatican.

9. The Dark Ages: Sometimes, historians call the first 400 to 500 years of the medieval ages, from A.D. 476 to about 900 or 1000, as the Dark Ages.

10. Polytheists: Polytheists are people who believe in many gods.

13. The Romanization of Europe

From the end of the **Roman Empire (A.D. 476)** to about the year 1000, one of the greatest and most rapid changes in history occurred. The various tribes of Europe went from being illiterate to literate, from living as tribes to living in organized kingdoms, from living as people ruled only by physical might to citizens living under the law. Chaos and violence gave way to order and peace. By 1000, for the average person in Europe, life, though not perfect, was much better than it had been.

One institution survived the fall of the Roman Empire—the Christian Church, centered in Rome, with the Pope as its head. Christians trace the beginning of their Church to Jesus choosing the Apostle Peter as the first leader of the Church. In the first century, Church Fathers called this the **Church universal**, because it was the first religion in the world that was open to all people of all nations. Universal translates from Greek into the word "**Catholic.**" This is why the early Christians called themselves Catholic.

Early Christians were fervent missionaries who wanted to spread the message of Christianity throughout the world. In medieval times, the chief missionaries to the pagan Germanic, Celtic, and Slavic tribes of Europe were monks. **Monks** were Christian men who devoted their lives to God and the Church, took vows of celibacy, spent their time working among the poor, teaching better methods of agriculture, and persuading pagan peoples to give up their faith and sometimes horrific practices, such as sacrificing humans. Monks ran hospitals and also preserved and promoted the best literature of the world by copying Latin script and teaching others.

Great missionaries went out to the pagan peoples and began the drastic change in the medieval world. **St. Patrick** (c. 387-493) was a Britain who had been imprisoned in Ireland by Celtic pirates. He escaped and returned to **Ireland** as a bishop and is attributed with converting the whole country. The Catholic Church still sends Irish priests throughout the world as missionaries. **St. Benedict of Nursia** (480-547), was the first to establish **monasteries**, thus setting up the system that would play an integral role in changing Europe. **St. Boniface** (c. 675-754), a missionary to the Germanic peoples, was killed by someone who rejected his missionary work. **St. Cyril and St. Methodius,** ninth century missionaries to the Slavic people, began the conversion of the Russians, Poles, Czechs, and Southern Slavs.

In addition to Christianity, Europeans saw the advantages of the Roman way of life in political, economic and cultural areas, and thus adopted Roman practices. Leaders in each nation learned how to read and write Latin, developed their own written language, created common legal systems, and established kingdoms that became the modern countries of Europe.

Facts to Know for The Romanization of Europe

1. End of the Roman Empire: The Roma Empire ended in A.D. 476.

2. Church universal: Early Christians called the Church universal, because it was the first religion open to all peoples of the world, not just to one nation.

3. Catholic: In Greek, Catholic means universal. This is why early Christians called themselves Catholic.

4. Monks: Monks were Christian men who devoted their lives to God and the Church.

5. St. Patrick: St. Patrick spread Christianity throughout Ireland.

6. Ireland: Ireland is an island west of Britain.

7. St. Benedict of Nursia: St. Benedict established the first monastery and spread Christianity among people in Italy.

8. Monasteries: Monasteries are where monks live and work. In medieval times, monasteries were also hospitals.

9. St. Boniface: St. Boniface was a missionary to the Germans.

10. St. Cyril and St. Methodius: These two Greek brothers were missionaries to the Slavic peoples.

14. Foundation of European Kingdoms

The modern nations of Europe trace their foundations to their medieval kingdoms. In every kingdom, Christianity played a key role in the foundation period. The Franks founded the first European kingdom in the fifth century. This later became the kingdoms of the French, the Germans, and the Italians. The kingdom of England was founded in the ninth century, followed by the Russian kingdom in the tenth and eleventh centuries. By 1200, all of the major European kingdoms had been founded, and the foundation for modern Europe had been set.

The **Franks**, a Germanic tribe occupying the area around modern-day Paris, France, began their kingdom in the fifth century. **Clovis I** converted to the faith of his wife, Catholic Christianity, and brought his nation into the same church. Clovis began the **Merovingian Dynasty**, which would lead the Frankish Empire for two centuries. (A **dynasty** is a ruling family.)

The next dynasty that ruled the Franks was the Carolingian. In 732, **Charles Martel (Charles the Hammer)** would lead the Franks in defeating the Muslim invaders of Europe, saving the continent from conversion to Islam at the **Battle of Tours**. His grandson, **Charlemagne** (Charles the Great), united much of central Europe, forcefully converting many of the European tribes. Charlemagne was crowned Holy Roman Emperor and tried to bring back the glory of Rome united with the Christian faith. Charlemagne encouraged learning in his empire and enforced strict adherence to Christianity throughout his realm. Charlemagne's three grandchildren became leaders of kingdoms that would eventually become France, Germany, and Italy.

King Alfred the Great founded the medieval kingdom of England by the ninth century. Alfred, the only English king called great, united the Angles and Saxons, established a Christian kingdom, defeated the pagan Vikings, and encouraged learning. Today, Queen Elizabeth II is a direct descendent of Alfred! For over 1,000 years one family has been English royalty.

Medieval Russia had been strongly influenced by Slavic and Viking pagan beliefs and practices until **St. Vladimir I** converted to Christianity around A.D. 1000. Prince Vladimir had lived a common pagan life, had many wives, and had erected shrines to Viking and Slavic gods. He then converted to Christianity, chose one wife, and converted so many Russians that he is called "Apostle of the Russians." He firmly established the **Eastern Orthodox Christian Church** (religion of the Eastern Roman Empire, also called Byzantium) in Russia.

Facts to Know for the Foundation of European Kingdoms

1. Franks: The Franks were a Germanic tribe occupying the area around modern-day Paris, France. They began their kingdom in the fifth century. They are the ancestors of the French.

2. Clovis I: Clovis I is the first King of the Franks, and began the Merovingian Dynasty. He converted to Catholic Christianity.

3. Battle of Tours: In 732 at the Battle of Tours, Charles the Hammer Martel defeated the Muslims who were trying to conquer Europe.

4. Charlemagne: Charlemagne was crowned Holy Roman Emperor in 800 and united much of Western Europe.

5. King Alfred the Great: King Alfred the Great united the Angles and Saxons and defended the English against the Vikings.

6. St. Vladimir I: St. Vladimir I is known as the Apostle to the Russians.

7. Eastern Orthodox Christian Church: The Eastern Orthodox Church was the official religion of the Eastern Roman Empire (also called Byzantium).

8. Charles Martel (Charles the Hammer): Charles Martel defeated the Muslims at the Battle of Tours in 732 and he was the grandfather of Charlemagne.

9. Merovingian Dynasty: The Merovingian Dynasty was the first Frankish Medieval dynasty.

10. Dynasty: Dynasty means a ruling family.

15. Medieval England and the Law

The principles of **liberty** and **limited government** developed in medieval England. Combined with ancient precedents, these principles later inspired the American Founding Fathers to create the first modern republic where citizens enjoy more rights than anywhere else in the world.

For centuries, families from Anglo-Saxon or Danish peoples ruled England. In 1066, **William of Normandy** invaded England, winning the Battle of Hastings, and made himself king. He established a feudal order that had already existed in all of Europe. The feudal order was based on the idea of exchanging land for loyalty and the idea that each person had obligations to the local lord and community.

Over the following centuries, the English established practices and laws that whittled away the power of the kings and the nobility. In the early 1200s, one of England's least popular kings, **King John**, tried to raise taxes on the lords and burghers (townsmen). The lords rebelled against him. Instead of handing more tax money to King John, in 1215 the lords forced the king to sign a document, called the **Magna Carta**, which limited his power.

The Magna Carta stated that if the king wanted to raise taxes, he had to ask permission of the lords and burghers. It gave nobles and burghers the right to "**due process of law**." Due process of law means that each person was guaranteed rights, such as a trial by jury, and that no government could take away these rights.

Medieval English judges established the principle of **common law**. A common law meant that all of England would follow the same law, instead of having local laws that varied in nature. This common law was not found in one written document, but in the oral traditions and decisions of English court cases. Common law established the idea that English law could not change at the whim of the leader. Common law is unwritten, passed on by judges in oral tradition.

In 1289, King Edward I assembled a group of nobles with the intention of having them vote for higher taxes to support a war. However, this initial meeting developed into the **English Parliament**, which became the body of men who create the law in England. Parliament has two houses, an upper house (House of Lords) which consists of church leaders and nobles, and a lower house (House of Commons) which consists of knights and local citizen leaders.

Constitutionalism is a set of ideas, attitudes, and behaviors based on the principle that the authority of government comes from a body of fundamental law. It means that government is limited by its laws and the practices of law and government over a period of time. A related concept, **the rule of law**, means that laws govern a country, not the opinions and whims of its rulers. Constitutionalism and the rule of law are two concepts that make it impossible for a ruler to take full control of a government.

Facts to Know for Medieval England and the Law

1. Liberty: Liberty refers to political rights that citizens in a free country have. Examples of liberty are the right to vote, the right of free speech, the right to choose one's own religion, and the right to own a gun.

2. Limited Government: Limited government refers to a government that exists to serve its citizens in limited ways, and therefore, it does not have much power.

3. William the Conqueror: William of Normandy invaded England in 1066 and became the King of England after winning the Battle of Hastings. William's army was the last to ever defeat the island.

4. King John: King John of England was very unpopular, and in fact, after him, there never was an English king named John.

5. Magna Carta: The Magna Carta, 1215, is a document that limited the power of the English king.

6. Due Process of Law: This term means that every citizen deserves to have the process of the law fairly administered.

7. Common Law: Common law meant that all of England would follow the same law, instead of having local laws that varied in nature.

8. English Parliament: In 1289, the English Parliament met for the first time. Parliament is a group of people who make laws.

9. Constitutionalism: Constitutionalism is a set of ideas, attitudes, and behaviors based on the principle that the authority of government comes from a body of fundamental law.

10. The Rule of Law: This concept means that laws govern a country, not the opinions and whims of its rulers.

16. The Crusades

In 1095, Pope Urban II called for a massive religious war. The **Crusades** were a series of wars that Christian Europeans waged against Muslim Turks to free the Holy Land from Islamic control. They became a culture-changing event that opened up the rest of the world to the Europeans, leading to the growth of business, the Renaissance, and the discovery of America. Within four centuries after the Crusades, the medieval ages ended, and Columbus' great discovery of America began the colonization of the New World. A part of this New World would become the United States of America.

Islam is a religion founded by Muhammad, a seventh century Arab. Followers of **Islam**, called Muslims, believe in one God to whom all must submit. Medieval Muslims believed that they were called by God to conquer and convert the world.

For over 1,000 years, **the Holy Land**, the area of greatest religious importance for Jews and Christians, was controlled by the Greeks and then the Romans. In the 600s, the Islamic Caliphate of the Arabs captured Jerusalem and the Holy Land from the Orthodox Christian **Eastern Roman Empire** (also known as Byzantium). In the early years of Islamic rule, the Arab Muslims allowed Christian pilgrims to travel safely to the Holy Land. **Turkish Muslims** then conquered the land, and did not allow Christian pilgrims safe travel. The Turks threatened Constantinople, the capital city of Byzantium, and wanted to eventually conquer all of Europe. Because of these events, **Pope Urban II** called for a Crusade to free the Holy Land from the Muslims and stop the threat to the rest of Europe.

The Crusaders failed to take and maintain control of the Holy Land, but they forced the Muslim leaders to allow Christian **pilgrims** to visit. Perhaps more importantly, Crusaders witnessed the beauty and splendor of Asia, tried Asian spices that made food taste much better, and brought home beautifully colored textiles that Europeans had never seen. Europeans became eager to establish trade with the East and bring the best of Asia to their homes.

As a result, trade between Asia and Europe grew, European coastal cities such as **Florence, Italy**, became wealthy, and the growing merchant class in Europe benefitted from the exchange. However, to obtain the riches from Asia, European merchants had to pay Arab and Asian middle men who traveled along the **Silk Road** from Far East Asia to the Mediterranean Sea. The Silk Road was the path traders took, bringing silk, spices, and textiles from China to the Near East and then into Europe. Europeans wanted a quicker and less expensive route to Asia. Thus, the **exploration age** of Europe was born, in part, out of the European desire to seek a quicker trade route to Asia.

Facts to Know for the Crusades

1. Crusades: The Crusades were a series of wars that Christian Europeans waged against Muslim Turks to free the Holy Land from Islamic control.

2. Islam: Islam is a religion and followers are called Muslims. Medieval Muslims believed God wanted them to conquer and convert the world.

3. The Holy Land: The Holy Land is the area of greatest religious importance for Jews and Christians. Christians from the Byzantine Empire held it until the 637, when Muslim Arabs conquered it.

4. Eastern Roman Empire: This empire is also called the Byzantine Empire. The Eastern Roman Empire controlled the Holy Land until Muslim Arabs took it in the 600s.

5. Turkish Muslims: Turkish Muslims conquered Jerusalem from Arab Muslims in 1077.

6. Pope Urban II: In 1095, Pope Urban II called for a holy war, a Crusade, against the Muslims to win back Jerusalem so that pilgrims could travel to the Holy Land.

7. Pilgrim: A pilgrim is somebody who makes a journey for a religious reason.

8. Florence, Italy: Florence is an Italian city that became wealthy because of trade with the rest of the Mediterranean world. The Renaissance started here.

9. The Silk Road: The Silk Road was a land trade route from China to Near Asia.

10. Exploration Age: During the Age of Exploration, Europeans explored the world, settled new lands, and opened up trade routes with other lands.

17. Aztecs, Incas, Maya

In North and South America, large civilizations formed during the early Medieval Ages. The Aztecs, Incas, and Mayas created organized societies that were **polytheistic**, built permanent structures, and developed complicated systems of agriculture and governance. As with many ancient and medieval people, religion played an important role in society. Each society had a ruling class, a leading religious leadership group, and a great majority of poor peasants who did not own their own land. Eventually, Spain conquered the Aztecs, Incas, and Mayas and these native peoples adopted most of the customs, traditions, and religion of the Spanish.

Machu Picchu is the site of Inca ruins dating to the 15th century. It is located in Peru in the Andes Mountains, 7,790 feet above sea level. For a reason unknown, Incas abandoned the city during the Spanish conquest in the 1500s. In 1911, American historian Hiram Bingham discovered it. The Inca Empire was the largest of pre-Columbian America. Incas believed in **Inti**, their sun god, and their emperor was the "son of the sun." It remains a mystery why the Incas abandoned Machu Picchu.

Maya Pyramids were built as religious structures or tombs for important leaders. The Maya practiced **human sacrifice** on top of their pyramids by extracting the beating heart of their victims. Maya developed the only writing system of pre-Columbian America. They played a ball game similar to soccer and basketball. The Maya civilization endured for over 2,000 years, ending when the Spanish Empire conquered the last Maya city in 1697.

The Maya were people of pre-Columbian America whose civilization spanned two thousand years. They were known for their knowledge of astronomy, art, architecture, and writing. The **Maya calendar** was very accurate, recording lunar and solar cycles, eclipses and movements of planets. The calendar was round and farmers used it to determine the best time of the year for planting and harvesting. The Maya solar year was more accurate than the Julian year used in Europe. The Maya calendar was closely tied to the Maya religion.

Also known as The Temple of the Feathered Serpent, **Quetzalcoatl (Ketzlko-attle) Temple** was built c. A.D. 200 and is located in present-day central Mexico. The temple is in the civilization called Teotihuacan, and no one knows exactly who the people were who built it. The Temple takes its name because of the feathered serpent representations that cover its sides. The ancient people who built the temple sacrificed over two hundred humans to dedicate the temple. Later, Aztecs claimed that these were Aztec ancestors.

Facts to Know for Aztecs, Incas, and Maya

1. polytheistic: This word means the believe in many gods. The Aztecs, Incas and Maya were polytheists.

2. Machu Picchu: This is a city high in the Andes Mountains where Incas used to live. It was abandoned in the 1500s.

3. Inti: This is the name of the sun god of the Incas.

4. Human sacrifice: Human sacrifice was practiced by the Incas and the Aztecs. They believed their gods required the blood of sacrificial humans.

5. Maya Calendar: The Maya developed a calendar that was more accurate than the Julian calendar used in Europe during the Medieval Ages.

6. Quetzalcoatl (Ketzlko-attle) Temple: This is the Temple of the Feathered Serpent, located in present-day Mexico. Aztecs claim that the temple was built by their ancestors.

18. Homes of Native Americans

In North America, Indians adapted to the climate they lived in. Their homes they lived reflected the unique geographical and climactic elements of their distinct regions. In the north, near the Arctic circle, Indians used the abundance of ice as insulation. On the Plains, the Indians used the products derived from the buffalo for their homes. In the Southwest, where it is hot and dry, cliffs and shade were utilized to stay cool. And, Indians used the heat of the sun to create and build with adobe bricks. Because the Native Americans lacked a written language when other civilizations did have writing, it is difficult to place them in prehistoric or ancient or medieval times. They are, in a way, a part of and not part of prehistory and ancient and medieval times.

A **tipi** was the home of Indians who lived on the Plains. **Plains Indians** were nomads, hunters who followed herds of buffalo as they roamed the open areas located in the middle of present-day America. Tipis were made of buffalo hide, and Indians painted symbols on the hides. Tipis were mobile, and within a few hours, Indians of an entire village could pack up and be on the move.

An **igloo** is a traditional type of temporary home or tent for the Inuit who live in the circumpolar region of the north. **Circumpolar** means an area around the pole, in this case, the North Pole. The word *iglu* comes from the Inuit language and means house. Igloos are domes made of individual blocks of ice that lean on each other. While outside temperatures could be as low as -49 degrees Fahrenheit, inside the igloo could be 61 degrees Fahrenheit. Igloos are still used today as temporary places to sleep.

In the Southwest of the modern United States of America, some Indians lived in **cliff dwellings** in the 12th and 13th centuries. Structures of the homes ranged from one-room storage rooms to villages of 150 rooms. At **Mesa Verde**, Colorado, Indians farmed on the flat land located above the homes, and climbed down to the shady dwellings below the cliff's edge. While temperatures on the top of the cliff could be above 100 degrees Fahrenheit, in an underground room of the cliff dwelling, it remained 50 degrees Fahrenheit all year round.

In Spanish, pueblo means village or town. In the Southwest of the modern United States of America, **Pueblo** refers to a settlement made of adobe and wood as well as to Indian people that still live there today. Pueblo structures are multi-storied buildings with thick walls surrounding an open plaza. Ladders lowered from inside the building allow for entrance. Some Pueblo Indians live in pueblos today.

Facts to Know for Homes of Native Americans

1. Tipi: A tipi was the home of Native Americans of the Plains. It was made of buffalo hide.

2. Plains Indians: These were nomads who hunted and followed the buffalo herds on the American Plains.

3. Igloo: An igloo is a home made of ice that the Inuit lived in.

4. Circumpolar: This word means the area around one of the poles.

5. Cliff Dwellings: Indians of the Southwest lived in areas directly below a cliff.

6. Mesa Verde: This area is a well-known location of cliff dwellings in present-day Colorado.

7. Pueblo: This word means a settlement made of adobe and wood in the Southwest and also refers to Native Americans who still live in these today.

19. Technology

During the Medieval Ages, humans developed advancements in architecture, ship building, navigation, math, philosophy, warfare, and in all human activities. Technology had a significant impact on society.

We do not know exactly when the first **compass** was made, but at least as far back as the second century B.C., the Ancient Chinese used a compass for maintaining harmony in the home and for telling the future. They believed that if a person placed his home or business in the right direction, then his physical and mental health would be best. Europeans used the compass to help them with navigation.

The **astrolabe** is an instrument used for locating stars and planets, for telling time, and for surveying land, and it can be used at night. The "**mariner's astrolabe**" was used to determine latitude on the ocean. Navigators who travelled the globe during the **Age of Discovery** (15th – 18th century) needed the mariner's astrolabe to navigate on the open ocean. The astrolabe was invented in ancient Greece by **Apollonius of Perga** c. 200 B.C.

The **trebuchet** is a type of catapult that uses gravity or traction to throw an object that can destroy things. Medieval trebuchet could throw projectiles that weighed up to 350 pounds and was used in medieval warfare as a siege weapon to demolish buildings. A **siege** is when the military surrounds a city and cuts off supplies entering the city. The trebuchet was used from ancient times through the 1500s. The invention of **gunpowder** made the trebuchet obsolete.

The **caravel** is the type of ship that Christopher Columbus used to sail across the Atlantic Ocean and discover

America in 1492. The caravel is small, fast, sturdy and highly maneuverable. It can navigate shallow river waters, and sail into the wind (called beating). It was developed by **Prince Henry the Navigator** and became the favorite vessel of explorers.

Facts to Know for Technology

1. Compass: It is believed the ancient Greeks made the first compass, the Chinese later used the compass to keep harmony in their home, and the Europeans used it for navigation.

2. Astrolabe: This is an instrument used for locating stars and planets, for telling time, and for surveying land, and it can be used at night.

3. The Age of Discovery: From the 15th to the 18th centuries, Europeans explored and mapped most of the world.

4. Apollonius of Perga: It is thought that the Greek Apollonius invented the compass.

5. Trebuchet: This is a type of catapult that uses gravity or traction to throw an object that can destroy things. It was used in knocking down city walls and buildings.

6. Siege: This is when the military surrounds a city and cuts off supplies entering the city.

7. Gunpowder: The invention of gunpowder by the Chinese was used by the Europeans to explode things. Gunpowder made the trebuchet obsolete.

8. Caravel: This ship is small, fast, sturdy and highly maneuverable. It can navigate shallow river waters, and sail into the wind (called beating). It is the type of ship Columbus used to discover America.

9. Prince Henry the Navigator: This Portuguese supported sailors and developed the caravel.

10. Mariner's Astrolabe: This instrument allowed sailors to determine a ship's latitude.

20. Medieval Warriors

During the Medieval Ages, warriors from different civilizations played important roles not just in battle, but in society. In many instances, warriors made for a more peaceful society, protecting invaders from without. Sometimes, though, the warrior's primary purpose was to invade. Some combatants made religious vows, while some did not. Well-known among medieval combatants are the Vikings, the Mongol warriors, the Crusaders, and the Samurai.

The **Vikings** were Germanic Norse seafarers and farmers who raided and traded from Scandinavia throughout Europe and Asia during the late 8th through the 11th centuries. Highly effective warriors, Vikings traveled by **longship**, traversing incredibly far distances. They were pagans and worshipped Norse gods, such as **Odin and Thor**. The Vikings eventually became Christians and assimilated into the local populations.

The **Mongols** are an East-Central Asian people who built the world's largest empire during the medieval ages under **Genghis Khan** in the 13th century. Genghis Khan united the nomadic tribes of Northeast Asia and used the cavalry as an effective fighting force to conquer much of Asia and Europe. Genghis Khan is known for his brutal military campaigns, and the Mongols consider him the founding father of Mongolia.

From 1095 – 1291, Christians fought a series of wars against Muslims called the **Crusades.** In the 7th century, Arab Muslims conquered the Holy Land from the Christians. For centuries, Christians were allowed to take **pilgrimages** to sites where Jesus lived, such as Jerusalem.

Then, Turkish Muslims conquered the Holy Land, threatening the Byzantine Empire, and would not allow Christian pilgrims safe passage. **Crusaders** were Christian holy warriors who fought in the Crusades. Many wore a symbolic cross on their clothing. The Crusades concluded with Christians earning safe pilgrimage to the Holy Land, and Muslims holding all land.

Samurai were the military officers of medieval and early-modern Japan. Similar to the medieval European knight, the samurai served their lord and followed a strict code of honor, called **bushido**. The samurai were expected to exhibit high levels of self-discipline and duty. If a samurai was in danger of falling into the hands of the enemy, or if he had committed a serious offense, he would commit seppuku, by thrusting a blade into his abdomen, then drawing the blade from the left to the right. Zen Buddhism philosophy influenced the samurai.

Facts to Know for Medieval Warriors

1. Vikings: These were Germanic Norse seafarers and farmers who raided and traded from Scandinavia throughout Europe and Asia during the late 8th through the 11th centuries.

2. Longship: Vikings used a longship to traverse across long distances, with seamen powering the ship with oars.

3. Odin and Thor: These were two important Viking gods. Odin was considered the leader of the Viking gods.

4. Mongols: These are an East-Central Asian people who built the world's largest empire during the medieval ages.

5. Genghis Khan: This Mongol united the nomadic tribes of Northeast Asia and used the cavalry as an effective fighting force to conquer much of Asia and Europe. Cavalry means horse-mounted soldiers.

6. Crusades: These were a series of wars between 1095-1291 Christians fought against Muslim to try to win back the Holy Land.

7. Pilgrimage: A pilgrimage is trip that someone takes for religious reasons. Somebody on a pilgrimage is a pilgrim.

8. Crusaders: These were Christian holy warriors who fought in the Crusades. Many wore a symbolic cross on their clothing.

9. Samurai: These were the military officers of medieval and early-modern Japan.

10. Bushido: This was the strict honor code the Samurai lived under.

21. Royal Power

During the Medieval Ages in Europe, there was a belief that the king was the servant of God, chosen by Him to rule. The power of the crown was represented by the king. The power of the Church was represented by the Pope. These two powers worked together to maintain order and justice in society. Charlemagne and King Richard the Lionheart stand out as unique kings of the Medieval Ages.

Charlemagne (748-814), also known as Charles the Great, was a Frank who became the first emperor of the **Holy Roman Empire**. He had a dream to unite Western Europe in one Christian Empire, as it was united in the Roman Empire. Charlemagne conquered many peoples of Europe and forced those he conquered to become Christian or be executed. He had at least 18 children with his ten wives or concubines. After his death, his empire split into various kingdoms.

The castle in medieval Europe was used as a defensive structure for protection and safe haven in case of attack. Surrounded by strong, stone walls, the castle usually was built atop a hill or mountain to make it difficult to conquer. Each castle had a well for water, and supplies for food to last many months. Many castles had a **moat**, a body of water that surrounded the castle, with a **drawbridge** that lowered to allow people to walk over the moat into the castle.

The **Crown** is the royal headgear reserved for the king. It represents power, legitimacy, honor, glory, and triumph. When a medieval leader was proclaimed king, a crown was set upon his head. Crowns often contained jewels, and on top of the crown was a cross, or a decorative cross. This symbolized that the king received the blessing from God and the Church.

King Richard the Lionheart (1157-1199) was King of England from 1189-1199. He was given the name Lionheart because he was a fierce warrior and fought "like a lion." His mother raised Richard in France. He composed poetry and was known for his physical beauty, height, and strength. Richard spent only 6 months of his 10-year reign in England, due to fighting the Crusades in the Holy Land and residing in France. The legend of **Robin Hood** is about King Richard's absence.

Facts to Know for Royal Power

1. Charlemagne: He lived from 748-814 and was also known as Charles the Great in English. He was a Frank who became the first emperor of the Holy Roman Empire.

2. Holy Roman Empire: This was a loose confederation of medieval kingdoms and territories united under one emperor. It lasted from 800 to 1803.

3. Moat: Around many castles was a body of water so that invaders would have a more difficult time attacking the castle.

4. Drawbridge: It was common to have a bridge that could be drawn up into the castle wall so that invaders would not have easy access into a castle.

5. Crown: The crown is the royal headgear reserved for the king. When used in a sentence capitalized, such as "The Crown," it also refers to all the power a king had.

6. King Richard the Lionheart: He was King of England from 1189-1199 and fought for most of his reign in the Crusades.

7. Robin Hood: Robin Hood may be a legend or he may have existed. During King Richard's reign when he was in the Crusades, England was ruled by Richard's brother John, who is supposed to have heavily taxed the people.

22. Medieval Warfare

Medieval warfare in Europe changed over time, with the introduction of new weapons, such as the cannon, the longbow, and the ability of kings to train peasants as archers. But, during most of the medieval ages, battles were fought by knights, engaged in hand-to-hand combat that lasted but a few minutes. Leaders followed the teachings of the Catholic Church, which forbade fighting during the harvest season, on holidays, and during winter.

A **knight** was a soldier, clad in armor, who usually fought on horseback for a lord. He was responsible as a **landlord** and managed serfs who worked the land. In return for the land he received from his lord, he promised a certain number of days he would fight per year. Knights were trained over many years, beginning as a page, then a squire helping another knight with his weapons, gear, and everything needed to prepare for battle. Knights followed a **code of chivalry**, where they promised to be loyal, honest, and to not abuse his power over serfs.

A **joust** was a competition between knights on horses. The aim of the knight on horseback was to knock his opponent off his horse with a lance. Jousting replicated a clash of heavy cavalry on the battlefield, and was seen initially as training for war. The winner of the joust was revered as the most capable knight of the tournament. After the 14th century, jousting existed primarily as a sport. It was popular in the Middle Ages from about 1250 to 1600.

The **coat of arms** is a design on a shield that is a symbol used to identify an individual person or family, corporation, or state. Beginning c. the 11th century in Europe, coats of arms have been used by nobles, citizens, warriors, and kingdoms on shields and flags throughout Europe. No official regulations exist, though strong traditions of **heraldry** have governed how coats of arms are made and used.

A **cannon** is a large gun that uses gunpowder to launch a projectile (often a ball) that will either kill people or destroy buildings. The cannon was invented in China and later spread to the Islamic world and Europe in the medieval ages. Cannon was used to destroy castle walls or forts. To counter the cannon threat, star forts were developed, which made it difficult to shoot cannon straight into the wall.

The **longbow** was a weapon that brought the end of the medieval ages. It was over 6 feet tall, and required a very strong man to pull it. Incredibly, it could shoot an arrow from 450 to 1,000 feet with accuracy. The arrow shot from a longbow could pierce armor. Because the archer did not require armor or a horse, any man could be trained to shoot the longbow. The introduction of the longbow into battle made it possible for a king to hire his army and not have to use so many knights. This helped bring about the end of the Medieval Ages, as the importance of the knight dwindled. Kings could pay archers in coin and did not have to base the archer's salary in land.

Facts to Know for Medieval Warfare

1. Knight: He was a soldier, clad in armor, who usually fought on horseback for a lord.

2. Landlord: He owned land and rented it to others. He had more rights than most other subjects in a kingdom.

3. Code of Chivalry: This was an honor code medieval knights lived by.

4. Joust: This was a competition between knights on horses.

5. Coat of Arms: This is a design on a shield that is a symbol used to identify an individual person or family, corporation, or state.

6. Heraldry: This is the system by which coats of arms are devised, described, and regulated.

7. Cannon: This is a large gun that uses gunpowder to launch a projectile (often a ball) that will either kill people or destroy buildings. It came into use in the Medieval Ages around the 12th century in China and the 14th century in Europe.

8. Longbow: This was a very powerful bow weapon that shot arrows that could pierce armor.

23. Four Interesting Medieval People

Joan of Arc, a teenage French peasant girl, led the French army successfully against the British in the **Hundred Years War** (1337-1453). While in prayer, Joan believed she saw visions of and heard the voices of Archangel Michael, Saint Ann and Saint Barbara commanding her to lead the French in battle. Joan's success leading men in battle was a major reason for French King Charles VII's coronation. Joan was captured and turned over to the British, who tried her for heresy and burned her at the stake. The Catholic Church later proclaimed her a saint.

In the 5th century, **Attila** led the Huns in a wide-ranging invasion of Asia and Europe. The Huns were Asian nomads and capable horsemen. Attila's army destroyed enemy settlements and ravaged populations. In the fifth century, the capital city of the Christian Church was the Vatican in Rome and **Pope Leo III** was seen as the leader of the Christians. Both on horseback, the Pope and Attila the Hun met each other outside of Vatican City. No recording was made of what they said, but Attila did not attack and conquer the Pope and Vatican City.

Robin Hood is a mythical character who may have lived during the reign of King Richard the Lionheart (1189-1199) when the king was fighting in the Crusades. As the story goes, the man who ruled England raised taxes, and life was hard for everyone who was not a governmental employee. Robin Hood stole from the government and gave to the poor. Robin Hood is supposed to have been a great archer who lived in Sherwood Forest with a band of merry men.

Sir Thomas More (1478-1535) was an author, a lawyer, councilor to King Henry VIII, and Lord Chancellor of

England. **King Henry VIII** wanted a divorce, so he separated from the Catholic Church, and founded the Church of England, declaring himself as the Supreme Head of the Church of England. When Sir Thomas More would not take an **Oath of Supremacy** to honor King Henry VIII, the king had More tried and beheaded for treason. More also wrote *Utopia*, a book about an imaginary, perfect country. The Catholic Church declared him a saint.

Facts to Know for Four Interesting Medieval People

1. Joan of Arc: She was an illiterate teenage French peasant girl who led the French army successfully against the British in the Hundred Years War.

2. Hundred Years War: From 1337-1453 the Kingdom of England fought the Kingdom of England in this war.

3. Attila the Hun: In the fifth century, this Asian warrior conquered much of Asia and Europe.

4. Pope Leo the III: Also called Leo the Great, this Pope met Attila and stopped him from invading the Catholic Church leaders after Attila had conquered Rome.

5. Robin Hood: He is most likely a mythical character who lived during the reign of King Richard the Lionheart (1189-1199) when the king was fighting in the Crusades.

6. Sir Thomas More: He lived from 1478-1535, was an author, a lawyer, councilor to King Henry VIII, and Lord Chancellor of England. King Henry VIII had Sir Thomas More executed.

7. King Henry VIII: In the 16th century, King Henry VIII of England made himself head of the Church in England and outlawed the Catholic Church.

8. Oath of Supremacy: In the 16th century, King Henry VIII made all of England take this oath that proclaimed King Henry VIII head of the Christian Church in England.

24. Famous Medieval Leaders

King Don Pelayo was a Christian Visigoth who began the "**Reconquista**" of Spain from Muslim power. From 711 – 788, Muslims invaded and conquered Hispania (later called Spain). Muslims established an Islamic caliphate in Spain and treated all non-Muslims as second-class citizens. Pelayo founded the kingdom of Asturias and began the Reconquista, the Christian reconquest of Spain from the Muslims.

Saint Wenceslas was a tenth century (c. 907-935) Duke of Bohemia who lived an extremely good Christian life. Wenceslas was **martyred** (killed for his faith) by his brother Boleslav and a group of noblemen. In the medieval ages, it was common for ruling members in the same family to kill each other for power. As Wenceslas was being killed, he said words of forgiveness towards his brother. He is the Czech patron saint and inspired the Christmas song "Good King Wenceslas."

Vladimir the Great (958-1015) was a prince of the Rurik Dynasty who became ruler of Kievan Russia. The **Rurik Dynasty** was a family of Scandinavian and Slavic descent who ruled Russia until 1598, when the Romanovs took over. Vladimir was initially a pagan with many wives and 800 concubines. He converted to Christianity, joined the **Eastern Orthodox Church**, and converted much of Russia. The Roman Catholic and Eastern Orthodox Churches proclaimed him a saint.

Alfred the Great was the first king of the Anglo-Saxons and the only English king to be called "great." He lived from 849 to 899 and successfully united and defended the English kingdom from the Vikings. Alfred was an educated man with the reputation of a merciful and level-headed ruler. For these reasons, Alfred greatly differs from many other medieval rulers. King Alfred reorganized the military, the taxation, the navy, education, and the laws of early England.

Facts to Know for Famous Medieval Leaders

1. King Don Pelayo: He was a Christian Visigoth of the 8th century who began the "Reconquista" of Spain from Muslim power.

2. Reconquista: This was the name given to the nearly 800-year war the Spanish fought against the Muslims in Spain, called the Moors.

3. Saint Wenceslas: He was a tenth century Duke of Bohemia who lived an extremely good Christian life and is the patron saint of the Czechs.

4. Martyred: When someone is killed because of his faith, he is a martyr. The past tense of martyr is martyred.

5. Vladimir the Great: He was a prince of the Rurik Dynasty who became ruler of Kievan Russia from 985 to 1010.

6. The Rurik Dynasty: This was a family of Scandinavian and Slavic descent who ruled Russia until 1598, when the Romanovs took over.

7. Eastern Orthodox Church: This is a Christian Church which split from the Roman Catholic Church in 1054. Many Slavs belong to the Eastern Orthodox Church.

8. Alfred the Great: He was the first king of the Anglo-Saxons and the only English king to be called "great." He lived from 849 to 899.

25. A Review of The Medieval Ages

The events and people of medieval history greatly influenced the foundation and history of the United States of America. From the time the Roman Empire collapsed in **A.D. 476** to the **discovery of America in 1492,** the civilizations that would establish the United States went through great changes.

The Dark Ages in medieval Europe refers to the period between the 5th and 10th centuries. During this time, **barbarian** Germanic, Slavic, and Celtic societies were transformed. In the 5th century, these peoples were pagan, some practiced human sacrifice, and most were illiterate. These ancient tribes conquered and ruled where the Roman Empire had once dominated. **Christian missionaries** from the Roman Catholic Church, such as Saint Benedict, Saint Boniface, and Saint Patrick converted the pagan Europeans to Christianity. Because of the actions of the Church, the newly converted European Christians adopted Roman systems of government and law, and began to establish higher institutions of learning. The modern people of Europe were born during the first five centuries of the medieval ages.

From 1000 to 1500, Europeans established complex societies, banking systems, the beginning of capitalism, higher forms of art and literature, and invented and developed a high level of technology in many areas. Europeans rediscovered cultural advances of the ancient world and had a rebirth of interest in classical life during a period called the **Renaissance**. Adventurers and leaders were excited to discover new lands and to acquire riches. And, in 1492, Catholic Spain completed the **Reconquista,** or reconquering, taking Spain back from the Muslims who had controlled Spain since the 700s.

In 1492, Europeans, and especially Spaniards, were eager to spread the Christian faith, open up new markets, and explore the world. Spanish **King Ferdinand and Queen Isabella** agreed to sponsor Genoese explorer Christopher Columbus to seek a faster passage to Asia. Though Columbus believed he found India, instead, he opened up colonization of North and South America to all the European countries. The British established 13 English colonies in America, and these would later become the United States of America.

Throughout the medieval ages in England, the English people incrementally limited the power of the king and of the government. The English thought that the less power the government had, the more liberty the people could enjoy. In 1215, King John was forced to sign the **Magna Carta**. The Magna Carta limited the power of the monarch and granted rights to noblemen. In 1289, **Parliament** was formed. Parliament is made up of representatives and it has the power to pass laws. In 1689, Parliament passed the **English Bill of Rights**, which guaranteed liberties to English citizens. When the Americans established their republic, they drew from hundreds of years of an English government that was limited in power. Because of medieval history, when Americans formed the United States of America, their intent was to create a government that had as few powers as necessary in order to guarantee rights to the individuals.

Facts to Know for Review of the Medieval Ages

1. Dates of the Medieval Ages: The Medieval Ages were from c. A.D. 476 to 1492.

2. Discovery of America: In 1492, Columbus discovered America.

3. Barbarian: Romans called pagan peoples they believed were backwards "barbarians."

4. Christian missionaries: Christian missionaries converted pagan barbarians to Christianity.

5. Renaissance: Europeans rediscovered cultural advances of the ancient world and had a rebirth of interest in classical life during a period called the Renaissance.

6. Reconquista: Catholic Spain retook land Muslims had conquered, ending the 700-year war in 1492.

7. King Ferdinand and Queen Isabella: These Spanish leaders completed the Reconquista and commissioned Columbus to find a new route to Asia.

8. Magna Carta: Signed in 1215, the Magna Carta limited the power of the English monarch and granted rights to noblemen.

9. Parliament: Beginning in 1289 in England, Parliament is made up of representatives and it has the power to pass laws.

10. English Bill or Rights: Passed in 1689, the English Bill of Rights guaranteed individual rights of all Englishmen.

Part II
Early Modern and Modern World History

26. The Renaissance

The **Renaissance** marks the end of the Middle Ages and the beginning of the Modern Period. During the Middle Ages, Europeans saw themselves as members of a community. In the Modern Period, they came to see themselves as individuals. The Renaissance changed the Europeans' view of the world, especially their view of God, religion, and themselves.

Beginning in **Florence, Italy** in the 1300s and spreading throughout Europe for the next two centuries, the Renaissance was a "rebirth" of interest in Classical Greek and Roman thought and culture. During the Renaissance, Europeans elevated the importance of nature, literature, human emotions, and **realism** (representing subject matter truthfully). They changed from writing only in Latin to the **vernacular** (the everyday language of their communities). They believed that studying the writings of classical Greeks and Roman could help them become better people and better Christians

After the fall of the Western Roman Empire (**A.D. 476**), Europe entered into the Middle Ages and for several centuries was ruled by various illiterate and barbarian tribes. The Roman Catholic Church converted (Christianized) the Europeans and from about the eighth century on controlled the cultural life of Europeans. The church directed society to focus on worshipping God. It created a system of education for the upper classes called scholasticism. **Scholasticism** was a practical form of education that focused on teaching religion and subjects such as logic and science. The church shunned or ignored non-Christian authors such as the ancient Romans and Greeks.

During the Crusades (**1095-1291**), Europeans increased their trade with the outside world, trading with Asia. In the city-states of Italy on the coast of the Mediterranean, a growing merchant class was achieving great economic success for example. Their trading brought new ideas from trading partners such as the Eastern Roman Empire, centered in **Constantinople**. Unlike the rest of Europe, scholars from the Eastern Roman empire were educated in ancient Greek and Roman culture as well as Christianity and the sciences. Increased wealth gave Italy's growing merchant class time to study topics outside of religion and the sciences, such as the human condition (human needs and desires) found in Greek and Roman literature.

Once introduced to the authors of ancient Greece and Rome, the educated people of Florence were captivated with the thoughts of the ancient Greeks and Romans. Europeans tried to create beautiful works of art and architecture, write in the vernacular, and improve knowledge of science in order to glorify God. Historians call this **Renaissance Humanism**. At this time, Muslim Ottomans were threatening to conquer Constantinople, which was the last remnant (part) of the Eastern Roman Empire. The Ottomans accomplished this in **1453** bringing the final end to the once glorious Roman Empire. The Ottomans renamed Constantinople Istanbul. Over the next half century, Greek professors continued to flee Constantinople with ancient Greek and Latin manuscripts that they brought to the University in Florence.

The Renaissance movement spread throughout Italy and the rest of Europe and resulted in Europeans emulating (imitating) ancient Greek and Roman art, architecture, and literature. By the 15th century, the Renaissance had spread to Northern Europe, and Europe had rediscovered the great works of classical Greece and Rome.

Facts to Know for The Renaissance

1. Renaissance: The Renaissance was a rebirth of interest in works and culture from classical Greece and Rome. Europeans emulated these works and created new art forms, architectural styles, and literature. It occurred between 1300 – 1700.

2. Florence, Italy: Florence was the Italian town where the Renaissance began.

3. Realism: In realism, artists try to representing subject matter truthfully.

4. Vernacular: The vernacular is the everyday language.

5. A.D. 476: In A.D. 476, the Roman Empire ceased to exist, and historians mark this date as the beginning of the Medieval Ages.

6. 1095-1291: European Christians fought Turkish Muslims during the Crusades, from 1095-1291.

7. Renaissance Humanism: During the Renaissance, Europeans tried to create beautiful works of art and architecture, write in the vernacular, and improve knowledge of science in order to glorify God.

8. 1453: In 1453, Turkish Muslims conquered the Eastern Roman Empire, also known as Byzantium.

9. Constantinople: Constantinople was the capital city of the Eastern Roman Empire.

10. Istanbul: After the Ottoman Turks conquered the Eastern Roman Empire, they renamed Constantinople Istanbul.

27. Beginning of the Renaissance

Renaissance means "rebirth" in French and refers to Europe from about 1300-1500. Europeans became interested in Classical Greece and Rome. They created works that glorified the individual and nature and not only religion. The Renaissance affected education, the arts, science, religion, and nearly every aspect of life in Europe.

Francesco Petrarch (1304-1374), was a Florentine (from Florence) lawyer and cleric who spent much time reading and writing poetry and essays. Petrarch thought that his own era – what he termed the "middle years" - offered no great examples of a good person. Instead, he admired ancient people, such as St. Augustine and Cicero, and thought that the ancients should be studied and emulated. Petrarch promoted the idea of Humanism, now known as Renaissance Humanism.

Renaissance Humanism in the 1300s meant classical scholarship – the ability to read, understand, analyze, and to emulate great Greeks and Romans. The Humanists were teachers of speaking and writing, called rhetoricians. They felt that by appreciating the writings of the ancient world they could learn the wisdom they needed to choose the right way in life and give glory to God. Humanists sought the highest virtues from the Church Fathers and also from the greatest ancient pagan authors.

Giovanni Boccaccio (1313-1375), a Florentine and friend of Petrarch, agreed with Petrarch. He focused on ordinary people in society. His novel, *The Decameron*, was a frank discussion of adult relationships, aimed at amusement. It was a sharp contrast to literature in the Medieval Ages, which focused solely on God's providence.

Florentines decided that they would promote the study of the ancients. In 1396, they invited Greek scholar **Manuel Chrysoloras** (c.1350-1415) from Constantinople to teach Greek at the university. At this time, Muslim Ottomans were threatening to conquer the last remnant of the once glorious Roman Empire. Over the next half century, Greek professors continued to flee Constantinople with ancient Greek and Latin manuscripts and taught at the **University of Florence**.

This trend spread throughout Italy: scholars studied the ancients, improved speaking and writing skills, emulated ancient art, literature, and even copied politics and social values. By the 15th century, the great works of the classical world and the Church Fathers entered the entire western world for the first time since the fall of the Western Roman Empire in 476.

Classical education in the Renaissance sometimes followed the teachings of Petrarch but not always. Works of history became increasingly analytical. However, at times education stressed memorization of classics over analysis. The classically educated person also learned proper manners. *The Courtier* by Baldassare Castiglione (1478-1529) stressed good behavior.

During the Renaissance, artists and architects emulated Classical Greek and Roman art and created incredibly beautiful sculptures, paintings, and buildings. Masters such as Leonardo de Vinci, Michaelangelo, and Rafael beautified cities and homes with art that showed the glory and beauty of the human. Their work remains with us today as examples of amazing works of art.

Facts to Know for Beginning of the Renaissance

1. The Renaissance: Renaissance means "rebirth" in French and refers to Europe from about 1300-1500. Europeans became interested in Classical Greece and Rome. They created works that glorified the individual and nature and not only religion. The Renaissance affected education, the arts, science, religion, and nearly every aspect of life in Europe.

2. Francesco Petrarch: Petrarch (1304-1374) was a Florentine lawyer who admired the ancient Greek and Roman culture and wanted other Florentines to study and emulate classical works.

3. Renaissance Humanism: Renaissance Humanism in the 1300s meant classical scholarship – the ability to read, understand, analyze, and to emulate great Greeks and Romans.

4. Giovanni Boccaccio: Boccaccio (1313-1375) wrote *The Decameron*.

5. Manuel Chrysoloras: Florentines invited the Greek scholar Chrysoloras (c.1350-1415) from Constantinople to teach Greek at the University of Florence.

6. University of Florence: This university was the center of the beginning of the Renaissance.

7. *The Courtier*: *The Courtier* is a book by Baldassare Castiglione (1478-1529) that stressed good behavior and etiquette.

28. The Renaissance in the South

The Renaissance began in Florence, Italy, in about 1300 and spread to other prosperous Italian city-states that traded with the Mediterranean world. Artists applied the lessons of the humanists to their art. They emphasized nature, the human figure, beauty, and perspective. Artists looked to ancient Greece and Rome for inspiration. For the first time since ancient time, nude bodies were depicted. The **"Renaissance Man"** was one of many talents in the arts and literature.

Leonardo de Vinci (1452-1519) of Florence was a sculptor, architect, scientist, engineer, and painter. His most famous paintings are the Mona Lisa and The Last Supper. As military engineer of Florence, he designed the city's defenses. He designed plans for machineguns, airplanes, tanks, and helicopters, even though no engine existed to power these machines!

Michelangelo di Lodovico Buonarroti Simoni (1475-1564) of Florence was a painter, sculptor, architect, and poet. His two greatest patrons were Lorenzo de Medici, ruler of Florence, and Pope Julius II. He painted the Sistene Chapel in Rome, painting 10,000 square feet of Bible scenes in four years. His statues of David and the Pieta are world renown. He designed the great Dome of St. Peter's Basilica.

Filipo Brunelleschi (1377-1436) of Florence designed a huge dome for the cathedral in Florence. It was the first dome since the Roman times.

Donatello (1386-1466) of Florence was perhaps the greatest sculptor of the 15th century. Donatello sculpted two statues, St. Mark and St. George, in a style reminiscent of Roman classicism. This was the first time in over 1,000 years that a sculptor had shown statues to have human personalities. Donatello invented the art of "schiacciato," a sculpture raised from a flat surface. He also sculpted David, the first large-scale, free-standing nude statue of the Renaissance.

Raphael (1483–1520) was a master painter and architect. He is known for painting groups of important figures, such as his paintings of the School of Athens and Disputa. His themes were from the classical world and the religious world. He became the chief architect of St. Peter's Basilica. With Michelangelo and Leonardo de Vinci, he is known as being one of top three Renaissance painters.

Writers of the Renaissance wrote in the vernacular, not in Latin, and some wrote for recreation. Writing reflected common earthly themes, instead of religious ones. **Giovanni Boccaccio** (1313-1375) of Florence wrote *The Decameron*, a frank discussion of adult themes. **Niccolo Machiavelli** (1460-1527) of Florence wrote *The Prince,* a book how a strong ruler should seize and hold power. From Machiavelli we received the teaching, "The ends justifies the means." This means that a strong ruler should, or does, whatever it takes to get his goal. **Dante Alighieri** (1265-1321) of Florence wrote *The Divine Comedy* in Italian. Before this, all major works were written in Latin. It is a book detailing Dante's journey through hell, purgatory, and into heaven. Dante encounters hundreds of people along the way. **Vasari** (1511-1574) wrote the first book on the history of art, detailing the most influential artists of the Italian Renaissance. To this day, his book is used to understand Western painting.

Facts to Know for The Renaissance

1. Renaissance Man: The Renaissance Man was one of many talents in the arts and literature.

2. Leonardo de Vinci: Leonardo de Vinci (1452-1519) of Florence was a sculptor, architect, scientist, engineer, and painter. His most famous paintings are the Mona Lisa and The Last Supper.

3. Michelangelo: Michelangelo di Lodovico Buonarroti Simoni (1475-1564) of Florence was a painter, sculptor, architect, and poet. He painted the Sistene Chapel in Rome. His statues of David and the Pieta are world renown. He designed the great Dome of St. Peter's Basilica.

4. Brunelleschi: Fillipo Brunelleschi (1377-1436) of Florence designed a huge dome for the cathedral in Florence. It was the first dome since the Roman times.

5. Donatello: Donatello (1386-1466) of Florence sculpted two statues, St. Mark and St. George, in a style reminiscent of Roman classicism. He also sculpted David, the first large-scale, free-standing nude statue of the Renaissance.

6. Raphael: Raphael (1483–1520) known for painting groups of important figures, such as his paintings of the School of Athens and Disputa. He became the chief architect of St. Peter's Basilica.

7. Giovanni Boccaccio: Boccaccio (1313-1375) of Florence wrote *The Decameron*, a book about everyday relationships.

8. Niccolo Machiavelli: Machiavelli (1460-1527) of Florence wrote *The Prince,* a book how a strong ruler should seize and hold power. From Machiavelli we received the teaching, "The ends justifies the means."

9. Dante Alighieri: Dante (1265-1321) of Florence wrote *The Divine Comedy* in Italian.

10. Vasari: Vasari (1511-1574) wrote the first book on the history of art, detailing the most influential artists of the Italian Renaissance.

29. The Renaissance in the North

The Renaissance, the rebirth of classical thought and art that began in Florence, spread throughout Europe in the 14th and 17th centuries. In the North, the Renaissance is known for an invention, paintings, literature, and music.

Perhaps the most important invention of the Renaissance was the **Gutenberg Press** by German Johannes Gutenberg (c.1400-1468). Before this, writers copied literature by hand, a painfully slow process. Gutenberg invented movable type which used metal letters that could be arranged and rearranged to form words. A machine called a press held the letters in place while a paper was pressed over it. Gutenberg's method remained the main printing method for 400 years. The first book that was printed with this method was the **Gutenberg Bible**, made c. 1455. The Gutenberg Press enabled the ideas of the Renaissance to spread quickly throughout Europe.

Oil painting developed in the north. In Netherlands. Flemish painter **Jan Van Eyck** (1390-1441) perfected this art. Van Eyck produced a new look to painting that created paintings that were vivid in detail. He discovered that by boiling a solution of mixed piled glass, calcined bones (bones burned to ashes) and mineral pigments in linseed oil, he could create a painting that was vibrant in color and light. He kept this knowledge secret until a few years before his death. **Albrecht Durer** (1471-1528) is regarded as the best German artist of the Renaissance. He painted altarpieces, portraits and self-portraits, and copper engravings. He is perhaps the first entrepreneurial artist. He sold his paintings with his wife on the market. The paintings of Dutch **Rembrandt van Rijn** (1606-1669) could be the most recognizable of Northern European Renaissance artists. Rembrandt used vivid color and light and shadows. His paintings were of biblical and historical figures, and also featured ordinary people in portraits.

Writers during the Renaissance broke from tradition by writing in the vernacular instead of Latin, making fun of tradition and religion, attacking superstition, ridiculing medieval notions of chivalry, and focusing on individuals. Englishman **Geoffrey Chaucer** (1340-1400) wrote *The Canterbury Tales*, the story of a pilgrimage to the tomb of St. Tomas Becket at Canterbury. In his story, pilgrims tell stories that highlight the lives of individuals in humorous ways. Dutch writer **Desiderius Erasmus** (1466-1536) attacked superstition and ignorance. Erasmus favored a reform of the Church but was against its division. He wrote a Greek translation of the New Testament, and essays on theology, education, and philosophy.

Englishman **William Shakespeare** (1564-1616) was perhaps the greatest playwright of all time. He wrote of famous characters in history, such as *Julius Caesar* and *Henry V,* and he wrote of intriguing stories of love, murder, and humor in *Hamlet* and *Romeo and Juliet*.
In Spain, **Miguel de Cervantes** (1547-1616) wrote *Don Quixote*, a story of an older man who believes he is a middle-aged knight who must fight for noble causes. His servant is Sancho Panza. De Cervantes ridiculed romantic ideas, but at the same time, honored them.

The Renaissance in the north changed society in many ways. The Gutenburg Press allowed ideas to spread quickly. Artists created new methods to make vivid paintings, and writers penned comedic and moving plays and novels.

Facts to Know for The Renaissance in the North

1. The Renaissance: The Renaissance was the rebirth of classical thought and art that began in Florence, spread throughout Europe in the 14th and 17th centuries.

2. Gutenberg Press: Johannes Gutenberg created this machine. It had movable type which used metal letters that could be arranged and rearranged to form words. A machine called a press held the letters in place while a paper was pressed over it. It made copying much easier.

3. Gutenberg Bible: The Gutenberg Bible (c. 1455) is the first book made with the Gutenberg Press.

4. Jan Van Eyck: Flemish painter Jan Van Eyck (1390-1441) created a new type of look to painting from his development of oil painting, making his paintings vivid in color and detail.

5. Albrecht Durer: Albrecht Durer (1471-1528) is regarded as the best German artist of the Renaissance and is perhaps the world's first entrepreneurial artist.

6. Rembrandt van Rijn: Rembrandt (1606-1669) could be the most recognizable of Northern European Renaissance artists.

7. Geoffrey Chaucer: Englishman Geoffrey Chaucer (1340-1400) wrote the humorous *The Canterbury Tales*, the story of a pilgrimage to the tomb of St. Tomas Becket at Canterbury.

8. William Shakespeare: Englishman William Shakespeare (1564-1616) was perhaps the greatest playwright of all time. He wrote of famous characters in history, such as *Julius Caesar* and *Henry V,* and he wrote of intriguing

stories of love, murder, and humor in *Hamlet* and *Romeo and Juliet*.

9. Miguel de Cervantes: In Spain, Miguel de Cervantes (1547-1616) wrote *Don Quixote*, a story of an older man who believes he is a middle-aged knight who must fight for noble causes. His servant is Sancho Panza.

10. Desiderius Erasmus: Dutch writer Erasmus (1466-1536) attacked superstition and ignorance. Erasmus favored a reform of the Church but was against its division.

30. The Age of Exploration

In the 1400s-1700s, Western Europeans led the **Age of Exploration**, a time when explorers discovered and mapped the world. City-states in Italy grew wealthy from trade with the East through the Mediterranean Sea, and Western Europeans wanted to go directly to the East by ocean instead of by land. Spanish and Portuguese sailors led the exploration of the world. The sailors' original goal was to reach India and the Far East by going around Africa. Although today we can see how to go around the south of Africa (commonly referred to as the **Cape of Good Hope**), people of the 1400s did not know how big Africa was, and traveling into unknown places without any maps is always terrifying.

In Portugal, the son of the king built a home overlooking the ocean and formed a school where sailors learned how to read maps and sail the ocean, all with the goal of sailing around the southern part of Africa to go to Asia. Because of his dedication and accomplishments, he is called **Prince Henry the Navigator**. Prince Henry died in 1463, before any of his sailors had succeeded in rounding the southern tip of Africa. Still, his ideas and school caught the imagination of sailors around the world.

Within 34 years after the death of Prince Henry, not only did sailors sail around the southern tip of Africa, but they navigated to India and changed the center of trading power from the Turks on the Mediterranean to the Western Europeans on the Atlantic. In 1486, Portuguese explorer **Bartholomew Diaz** succeeded in sailing around the southern tip of Africa. In 1492, Genoese **Christopher Columbus** discovered America for Spain. In 1497, **Vasco de Gama** sailed to India and back to Portugal, bringing caskets of jewels, rich spices packaged in silk, and incredible textiles. From 1519-1522, an expedition led by Spaniard **Ferdinand Magellan circumnavigated** the world. Magellan was killed during the journey. To avoid conflicting claims of new lands, Portugal and Spain signed The Treaty of Tordesillas (1494) that split the world in two. An imaginary line of demarcation was drawn: Portugal received everything east of the line, and west of it got Spain. The Spanish continued to explore. Vasco Nunez de Balboa discovered the Isthmus and the Pacific Ocean in 1513. Working as an observer, Americus Vespucci wrote Spain had discovered a new continent. A German scholar read his ideas and drew a new world map, naming the new continents America.

Throughout the 1500s to the 1800s, the European countries of Holland, Great Britain, and France joined Spain and Portugal in exploring the world. Italian **John Cabot** explored North America for the English. The Spanish explored South America and the southern part of North America, establishing a huge empire and spreading the Catholic faith among native peoples. Holland, Great Britain, and France explored and established colonies in North America that would eventually become the United States of America and Canada. Many explorers searched in vain for a **Northwest Passage**, an all water-route through North America to the Pacific Ocean.

Facts to Know for The Age of Exploration

1. The Age of Exploration: From the 1400s through the 1700s, Western Europeans explored much of the world.

2. Cape of Good Hope: This cape is in southern Africa, and most consider it the furthest southern point of Africa, although it is not.

3. Prince Henry the Navigator: Prince Henry was a Portuguese who sponsored sailors, cartographers, and explorers to live, study, and begin their explorations from his home.

4. Bartholomew Diaz: In 1486, Portuguese explorer Bartholomew Diaz succeeded in sailing around the southern tip of Africa.

5. Christopher Columbus: In 1492, Genoese Christopher Columbus discovered America for Spain.

6. Ferdinand Magellan: From 1519-1522, an expedition led by Spaniard Ferdinand Magellan circumnavigated the world.

7. Circumnavigate: Circumnavigate means to sail around the world.

8. John Cabot: Italian Cabot explored North America for England.

9. The Northwest Passage: Europeans searched in vain for The Northwest Passage, an all water-route through North America to the Pacific Ocean.

10. Vasco de Gama: In 1497, Vasco de Gama sailed to India and back to Portugal, bringing caskets of jewels, rich spices packaged in silk, and incredible textiles.

31. The Reformation and Martin Luther

The **Reformation** was a religious movement in Europe from about 1520 to about 1648. Religious reformers led a movement to change the Catholic Church and to establish new Christian religions. Catholics and those who left the Church, called **Protestants**, fought religious wars that redrew the political map of Europe.

Many Europeans grew skeptical of the **Pope**, the leader of the Christian Church, in part because of corruption and disorder. At one time, there were three popes, called the **Great Schism of the West** (1378-1417). One of the Popes lived in Avignon, France, while the others were in Rome. Some clergy (priests) were corrupt and sought financial gain. They sold church offices (simony) or rewarded relatives with important positions (nepotism). Others sold dispensations to raise money. A **dispensation** allowed a group to forego close adherence to a church rule. Some priests had wives and children, even though they promised to not have relations with women. Church leaders encouraged believers to buy indulgences: to pay money to have one's sins forgiven.

In the Late Middle Ages, European princes paid taxes to the king and the Church in Rome. Princes didn't like this, and they were interested in how they could gain independence from the Pope and from the Holy Roman Emperor. The Reformation eventually allowed many princes to break from the Pope and the Holy Roman Empire, and these princes no longer had to send tax money to the Church.

Martin Luther (1483-1546) is the central figure of the Reformation. A German monk, Luther initially protested against the Church by reportedly nailing a list of grievances on a church door in Wittenburg. Known as the "**Ninety-**

Five Theses," Luther protested the wrongful sale of indulgences, the Church's teachings on salvation, the authority and corruption of the Church, celibacy of the priests, and taught the need for a more personal relationship with God. In 1520, **Pope Leo X** excommunicated him.

Luther taught: 1. faith alone suffices for salvation, 2. the Bible alone was the only guide to Christianity, and 3. Christians could interpret the Bible on their own. Luther established a new religion, known as the Lutheran Church. It was very similar to the old religion. He married a former nun and had six children. Luther translated the Bible into German. The printing press allowed the Bible, and his writings, to be widely disbursed. In his writings, he attacked certain parts of the Bible, taking out the Epistle of St. James. From then on, all Christians who accepted Luther's reforms were known as Protestants. Followers of the traditional Christian Church were known as Roman Catholic.

Much fighting took place as a result of the Reformation. German Peasants believed that the break from the Church also meant that nobles should relinquish their greater privileges and revolted. With Luther's support, the princes crushed the **Peasant Rebellion** and killed over 100,000. A civil war in Germany broke out between the Holy Roman Emperor who sided with the Catholic Church and many German princes who sided with Luther. It ended with the **Peace of Augsburg** (1555). It was decided that whichever religion the prince was, the people in his area would adopt that religion, as well.

Facts to Know for The Reformation and Martin Luther

1. The Reformation: From about 1520 to 1648, religious reformers led a movement to change the Catholic Church and to establish new Christian religions in Europe.

2. Protestant: Christians who sided with Martin Luther and disagreed with the Roman Catholic Church were called Protestants, because they protested the Church.

3. Pope: The Pope was the leader of the Christian Church in the West until the Reformation.

4. The Great Schism of the West: In the Great Schism of the West (1378-1417), three different people claimed to be the Pope.

5. Dispensation: A dispensation allowed a group to forego close adherence to a church rule. In the Medieval Ages, some dispensations could be bought.

6. Martin Luther: Martin Luther (1483-1546) is the central figure of the Reformation and led the Protestant Movement against the Catholic Church.

7. Ninety-Five Theses: It is believed that Martin Luther nailed a list of 95 grievances against the Catholic Church on the door of the church at Wittenburg.

8. Pope Leo X: Pope Leo X excommunicated Luther in 1520. To excommunicate someone means to kick him out of the Church.

9. Peasant Rebellion: After Luther broke from the Church, German peasants believed they should be released from serfdom and have freedom. Luther supported German princes as they defeated the peasants, killing 100,000.

10. Peace of Augsburg: In the Peace of Augsburg (1555) European leaders decided that whichever religion the prince was, the people in his area would adopt that religion, as well.

32. The Spread of the Reformation

The Reformation spread throughout Europe in the sixteenth century. Most known of the Protestant leaders were **Ulrich Zwingli** in Zurich, **John Calvin** in Basel, and **King Henry VIII of England**. Some radical reformers tried to alter society but were crushed. Wherever Protestantism spread, leaders set up a theocracy where no dissension was tolerated.

Ulrich Zwingli (1484-1531) of Zurich, Switzerland was a priest and humanist. He broke from the Catholic Church, rejected celibacy and the sacraments, and taught the importance of correct behavior. Zwingli established a tribunal with informers to ensure all acted correctly. Zwingli banished all rituals and outlawed any practice of Catholicism. He brought back the practice of public confession of sin.

John Calvin (1509-1564) was the second major figure after Luther. A layman in France, he fled to Basel, Switzerland after writing against the Catholic Church. In Basel, he wrote the "Institutes of the Christian Religion", a thoroughly-detailed apology of Protestantism. Calvin taught that Scripture alone was the authority for the Christian, and he believed in predestination. He taught that God predetermined who was saved (going to Heaven), called the elect, and who was damned. Calvin destroyed all icons, such as crucifixes, statues, sacred paintings, vestments, altars, confessionals, and stained-glass windows depicting saints.

Although Calvin taught predestination, he believed people were obligated to act in ways to make God happy. To enforce this, he established a very strict **theocracy** in Geneva, Switzerland, outlawing all other religions. There was no dancing, card playing, drinking, or braiding hair.

Each home was inspected twice a year by religious police. The **Censor** had to initial each page of a new book. The opposition was tortured and burned at the stake.

Throughout Europe, Calvin's ideas inspired the formation of other Churches. In Holland it was Dutch Reformed Church. In Scotland, **John Knox** formed the Presbyterian Church. French Calvinists were called **Huguenots**. English Calvinists were called Puritans.

In England, King Henry VIII (1509-1547), was unable to have a son with his Spanish wife Catherine. He unsuccessfully petitioned the Pope for an annulment. King Henry VIII broke from the Catholic Church and remarried, eventually marrying six times. (He beheaded two of his wives!) In 1534, the English Parliament issued the **Act of Supremacy** that made Henry the leader of the new Church of England.

A period of religious struggle ensued in England. King Henry VIII closed all monasteries, seized church land, and banned all Catholic practices. Hundreds were beheaded and many were hung, drawn, and quartered because they would not swear an oath to the King. After his Protestant son Edward VI's short rule, his daughter **Mary I** (1516-1568) tried to bring Catholicism back by force during her five years of rule. Trying and executing hundreds who would not convert back to Catholicism, she was given the name "Bloody Mary." After her rule, Henry's Protestant daughter **Elizabeth I** (1533-1603) ruled for almost 45 years. Elizabeth I successfully planted Protestantism in England. She banned all public Catholic practices, executed over a hundred Catholics, and imprisoned thousands to enforce the Act of Supremacy.

Facts to Know for The Spread of the Reformation

1. Ulrich Zwingli: Ulrich Zwingli (1484-1531) of Zurich, Switzerland established a theocracy (government ruled by religious) and spy system aimed at making everyone behave correctly.

2. John Calvin: John Calvin (1509-1564) established a theocracy in Basel, Switzerland and believed in predestination, the idea that God created people, knowing who will go to Heaven and who will go to Hell, regardless of one's actions.

3. King Henry VIII: King Henry VII (1509-1547) of England broke from the Catholic Church because the Pope would not grant him an annulment. He established the Church of England and eventually married six times. (He had two of his wives beheaded).

4. Theocracy: A theocracy is a government ruled by religious people implementing religion as law.

5. John Knox: Knox established the Presbyterian Church in Scotland.

6. Huguenots: Huguenots were French Calvinists.

7. Act of Supremacy: This law made the King of England the religious head of the Christian Church in England.

8. Mary I: Mary I (1516-1568) of England tried to reestablish the Catholic Church in England, and was called "Bloody Mary" by those who were against her because of her violent crackdown of Protestants.

9. Elizabeth I: Elizabeth I (1533-1603) of England successfully established Protestantism, violently cracking down against Catholics.

10. Censor: In Calvinist Geneva, the Censor had to approve of books by initializing each page.

33. The Catholic Reformation

During the time of the Reformation, the Catholic Church implemented reforms to purify the Church, called the **Catholic Reformation**. In the first half of the sixteenth century, the Catholic Church lost millions of European faithful to various Protestant Churches. Among the countries that remained Catholic, kings asserted a great deal of autonomy. The French king could choose the bishops and the Spanish set up their own Inquisition. The Catholic Church was hurt by its practices of simony, nepotism, wrongful sale of indulgences, and its failure to express clearly its doctrine of salvation.

The election of Pope Paul III (served 1534-1549) changed the course of Catholic history. He crusaded against Church abuses, appointed learned and able Cardinals, and called for the **Council of Trent (1545-1563).** The council was a meeting of world Catholic leaders that clarified Church teachings and renewed Catholic spiritualism.

The Council taught that Scripture and Church are the two authorities for Christian life. Luther had taught that Scripture alone was needed. The Council asserted that the human will is completely free and that salvation is from faith and actions. Luther had taught that man's will was limited because of his sinful nature, and that a person could not fully participate in his own salvation because of his fallen grace. Calvin had taught that man's salvation was predetermined and that he could do nothing for his own salvation.

The Council went against Luther in a number of ways. Luther had denied the human action of the writing of the **Scripture**. The Catholic Church stated that normal men were inspired by God to write the Scripture, and that God used their faculties to do so. The Council argued that all seven sacraments are channels of real grace, that Christ is present in the transubstantiation, and that priests and ceremonies are important. **Ritual** was stressed, and gorgeous decorations of churches were promoted.

The Catholic Church founded a **Roman Inquisition** to fight Protestantism and created an "**Index of Forbidden Books**," which outlawed the reading of heretical works. It forbade the sale of indulgences and improved the education of local priests.

In the sixteenth century, mysticism flourished in the Catholic Church. Mystics seek the Holy Trinity in a personal way, in prayer, without a priest. **Teresa of Avila** (1515-1582) is the most well-known female Catholic mystic. She established the **Order of the Carmelite Reform**, a contemplative order of nuns with convents throughout Spain. **Ignatius of Loyola** (1491-1556) is the most well-known male Catholic mystic. He founded the **Society of Jesus**, also called the Jesuits, and converted tens of thousands in Asia.

Facts to Know for The Catholic Reformation

1. The Catholic Reformation: The Catholic Reformation was a series of reforms Catholics implemented in their Church to purify their religion.

2. Council of Trent (1545-1563): The Council of Trent was a meeting of world Catholic leaders that clarified Church teachings and renewed Catholic spiritualism.

3. Scripture: Scripture is what Christians call the New Testament. They believe man wrote the Bible inspired by God.

4. Ritual: A ritual is a religious or solemn ceremony performed by a directed order of events.

5. Roman Inquisition: The Roman Inquisition was a system of tribunals established by the Catholic Church to try individuals of going against the Church. Those guilty could be handed over to the civil authorities to be tortured or killed.

6. Index of Forbidden Books: The Catholic Church created a list of books that had to be destroyed and that no one was allowed to read.

7. Teresa of Avila: Teresa of Avila (1515-1582) was a Spanish mystic who established on Order of nuns.

8. Order of the Carmelite Reform: Teresa of Avila established this contemplative order of nuns with convents throughout Spain.

9. Ignatius of Loyola: Ignatius of Loyola (1491-1556) is the most well-known male Catholic mystic.

10. The Society of Jesus: Also called the Jesuits, the Society of Jesus converted tens of thousands of Asians to Catholicism.

34. The Rise of Empires

Why did Europeans colonize in the 16th and 17th centuries? There were basically two main reasons: economics and religion. Many Europeans wanted to find gold, better trade routes to Asia, cheaper raw materials, and land to grow crops on. Other Europeans wanted to either spread their Christian religious belief or to find a place where they could worship without harassment.

Portugal, first in exploration, was first in establishing colonies. The Portuguese established colonies in South America, Africa and India. The Portuguese established its richest colony in Brazil. Portuguese settlers set up large estates and slaves worked the land. Today, Brazilian exhibits its Portuguese heritage through its customs and language. In Africa and Asia, Portugal set up small trading posts and did not intermingle with the native population. For part of the sixteenth century, Portugal dominated the European trade of goods coming from the East.

Spain became Europe's most powerful empire of the 16th and 17th centuries. Within 100 years of Columbus discovering America, Spain controlled most of South America, Central America, Southwest North America, and islands in the Pacific. The **conquistador** was a soldier, eager for adventure with a high level of confidence. Perhaps fewer than 1,000 conquistadors overran much of the Americas. **Cortez** conquered the Aztecs and **Pizarro** the Incas. Spanish culture mixed with native cultures. The Spanish intermarried with the natives. In New Spain, the culture, religion, language, and customs resembled those of Spain. Spain's missionaries accompanied the explorers and conquistadores and brought Catholicism and European customs to the natives. The Spanish established many firsts in the Americas, including the first college, hospital, and printing press. The **College of the Holy Cross** was established 1535. The Spanish introduced plants, trees, vegetables, horses, dogs and cattle.

France, **Holland**, and **Great Britain** explored and colonized, as well. France took control of eastern Canada and the Mississippi River Valley and called it New France. It set up trading posts in the Caribbean and in India. Holland claimed New Netherlands (New York), some Caribbean islands, parts of South Africa and South America, and parts of Indonesia. Great Britain replaced Spain as the greatest empire by the end of the 18th century. In a series of wars against the other colonizing powers, Great Britain won dominance in the 13 colonies in North America, Canada, India, New Netherlands, and islands in the Caribbean. Whereas the Spanish and French intermarried with natives, the English tended to either destroy the Indians or push them out.

Colonization affected both the mother country and the colony. In Europe, new colonies brought wealth and cities grew. The transfer of goods, ideas, and people between the Americas and Europe was called the **Columbian Exchange**. From America came new foods like the potato and corn, as well as tobacco. The colonists brought European culture and Christian religions to the Americas, Asia, and Africa. Western civilization was transplanted to much of the world. Native Americans had no immunity from the European diseases of chicken pox and small pox and these wiped out 90% of many tribes.

Facts to Know for The Rise of Empires

1. Portugal: The Portuguese were the first in exploration and established colonies in South America, Africa and India in the 1400s and 1500s.

2. Spain: Spain established colonies in South America, Central America, Southwest North America, and islands in the Pacific in the 1500s and 1600s.

3. Conquistador: Conquistador were Spanish soldiers, eager for adventure with a high level of confidence. They conquered the Aztecs, Incas, and Mayas.

4. Hernando Cortez: Cortez conquered the Aztecs.

5. Francisco Pizarro: Pizarro conquered the Incas.

6. College of the Holy Cross: The Spanish established this in 1555. It was one of the first colleges established in the Americas.

7. France: France took control of eastern Canada and the Mississippi River Valley and called it New France. It set up trading posts in the Caribbean and in India.

8. Holland: Holland claimed New Netherlands (New York), some Caribbean islands, parts of South Africa and South America, and parts of Indonesia.

9. Great Britain: Great Britain won dominance in the 13 colonies in North America, Canada, India, New Netherlands, and islands in the Caribbean. It became the greatest colonial power in the 1700s and 1800s.

10. The Columbian Exchange: The transfer of goods, ideas, and people between the Americas and Europe was called the Columbian Exchange. From America came new foods like the potato and corn, as well as tobacco. The colonists brought European culture and Christian religions to the Americas, Asia, and Africa.

35. The Commercial Revolution

In the 1500s - 1700s, new ways of thinking and acting regarding money led to what historians call the **Commercial Revolution**. Because of the Commercial Revolution, power in Europe shifted from Italy and the Mediterranean trade to the Atlantic coast countries, like Spain, France, Great Britain, Holland, and Portugal. Perhaps most important to the Commercial Revolution was capitalism. **Capitalism** is an outlook and behavior taken by people who freely make, buy, and sell goods. In capitalism, people take risks in the hopes of improving their financial situation. Money that is earned is called **profit**. Individuals who earn a profit reinvest for more profit. In capitalism, hard work and risk taking is rewarded. Individuals tend to work harder for themselves because they get to enjoy the benefit of their labor. Bankers are ready to loan people capital in the hopes that they will be repaid with interest.

Generally, material ambition became more accepted in European society. It had once been that all Christians were forbidden to earn interest from loaned money. Some elements in society were still against the drive for wealth, though, as William Shakespeare expressed in his play "The Merchant of Venice," set in 16th century Europe.

The idea of the **corporation** emerged: a legal entity that had the rights of an individual. A **joint-stock company** was one where business people could put their money together to raise huge amounts of capital. Each person bought stock in the company and owned a share of it. These large amounts of capital were used to fund large enterprises, take huge risks, and reap or lose great amounts of wealth. Insurance products came into existence that guaranteed business ventures.

Merchants used their money to build new businesses, like manufacturing things. Cloth manufacturing was one such business. In a company that worked as a "**domestic system**," weavers were paid to make cloth in their homes. Capitalists paid weavers with wages and raw materials. They then sold the goods in the market for a profit. Over time, they brought the raw materials and workers in one location, called the factory system.

Global trade increased the European standard of living, and the wealthy financed enterprises. Europeans invested in tobacco and sugar plantations in America and in coffee plantations in Asia. **Johannes Fugger** of Augsburg was the head of a very successful banking family. The Fuggers funded the quest of Spanish King Charles I (1500-1558) to become Holy Roman Emperor Charles V.

During the Commercial Revolution, kings tried to enrich their countries through the policy of mercantilism. **Mercantilism** was an economic theory where colonies existed only to enrich their founding country. Colonies sent raw materials to the home country. The home country made manufactured products and sold them back to the colonies. **Tariffs** were taxes on imported goods. Some argue that tariffs protect the home country's products.

In the middle of the Commercial Revolution, from 1470 to 1610, Europe's population grew over 50% and Europe experienced a warming climate. The **warming climate** allowed for better agricultural production. More farm laborers produced more food from the warmer environments. London grew from under 50,000 in 1500 to over 200,000 in 1600.

Facts to Know for The Commercial Revolution

1. Commercial Revolution: From the 1500s - 1700s, new ways of thinking and acting regarding money led to what historians call the Commercial Revolution. It involved capitalism, corporations, and the joint-stock company.

2. Capitalism: Capitalism is an outlook and behavior taken by people who freely make, buy, and sell goods.

3. Profit: In capitalism, people take risks in the hopes of improving their financial situation. Money that is earned is called profit.

4. Corporation: A corporation is a business that has the rights of an individual.

5. Joint-Stock Company: A joint-stock company is one where business people put their money together to raise huge amounts of capital. Each person buys a share/stock in the company and owns a share of it.

6. Domestic System: In a domestic system, weavers were paid to make cloth in their homes. Capitalists paid weavers with wages and raw materials. They then sold the goods in the market for a profit. It was called a domestic system because work was done in the home.

7. Johannes Fugger: Johannes Fugger of Augsburg was the head of a very successful banking family.

8. Mercantilism: Mercantilism was an economic theory where colonies existed only to enrich their founding country. Colonies sent raw materials to the home country. The home country made manufactured products and sold them back to the colonies.

9. Tariffs: Tariffs are taxes on imported goods. Some argue that tariffs protect the home country's products.

10. Warming Climate: From 1470 to 1610 there was a warming climate. This allowed for better agricultural production. More farm laborers produced more food from the warmer environments. London grew from under 50,000 in 1500 to over 200,000 in 1600.

36. Ruling Houses of Europe

During the Renaissance and Reformation (1300s-1500s), kings grew in importance and the old feudal order died. Ruling houses of England, France, and Spain encouraged trade, exploration, raised taxes, and tried to relieve social distresses. Dynasties created modern state bureaucracies. Many kings and queens enjoyed absolute power, taking charge over all political and religious affairs.

In England, the **Tudor Dynasty** established itself as a great power. **Henry VII** (ruled 1485-1509) increased the power of the gentry, landowners who were not nobility. He made the gentry Justices of the Peace who administrated his realm. He also created royal councilors (the Star Chamber) who ruled on legal issues without the need for a jury or having to follow common law.
King Henry VIII (ruled 1509-1547) destroyed the Scots at the Battle of Flodden 1513. He fought with France, broke from the Catholic Church, and established the Church of England. He imprisoned thousands and executed hundreds of Catholics. He had six wives, killing two of them. **Queen Elizabeth I** (ruled 1558-1603) established England as perhaps the mightiest nation in Europe. Known as "The Virgin Queen" because she never married, she ensured the strength of the Church of England, imprisoning thousands and executing hundreds of Catholics. Her navy defeated the Spanish Armada in 1588.

French kings expanded their empire through negotiation and force. In the 1400s, France was a large country with 15 million people. It had the most fertile land of Europe. Its kings promoted the sale of offices, and this encouraged corruption and the expansion of bureaucracies. A representative body called the Estates General existed, but it had less power than the English Parliament. **King Louis XI** (ruled 1461-1483) established the **Valois Dynasty**.

Called "The Spider", Louis XI grew his empire by negotiation and treaties instead of war. His son **Charles VIII** (ruled 1483-1498) was constantly at war with the Hapsburgs over northern Italy. Unlike England, France remained loyal to the Catholic Church. **King Francis I** (1515-1547) gained the power of investiture. He was able to choose who became bishops and cardinals, and thus, controlled the Church.

Queen Isabella I of Castille and King Ferdinand II of Aragon founded the Spanish kingdom in the 1400s, a country of 11 million. They were of the House of Trastamara (1479-1555). They defeated the Moors, finishing the 700-year war against the Muslims in 1492. They expanded Spain by commissioning Christopher Columbus to sail, and he discovered America. The king and queen enriched Spain and Europe by taking great amounts of silver and gold from native Americans. After defeating the Muslims in 1492, they expelled all 150,000 Jews from Spain. They created their own Inquisition and forcefully pursued suspected heretics. Spaniard mystics Saint Ignatius of Loyola and Saint Theresa of Avila founded new contemplative religious Orders. Isabella's grandson, **Charles I** (1516-1556), became Holy Roman Emperor in 1519, joining the Kingdom of Spain with the Habsburg Empire. He was constantly fighting wars in Europe to protect his realm and fighting the Protestants in religious wars. *All* of the current monarchs in Europe (in 2017) are descendants of Queen Isabella I and King Ferdinand II.

Facts to Know for Ruling Houses of Europe

1. Tudor Dynasty: From 1485-1603, the Tudors established England as one of the world's great powers.

2. Henry VII: Henry VII (ruled England 1485-1509) increased the power of the king and created royal councilors (the Star Chamber) who ruled on legal issues without the need for a jury or having to follow common law.

3. Henry VIII: He ruled England 1509-1547 and destroyed the Scots at the Battle of Flodden 1513. He established the Church of England, imprisoning thousands and executed hundreds of Catholics. He had six wives, killing two of them.

4. Queen Elizabeth I: Queen Elizabeth I (ruled England1558-1603) was known as "The Virgin Queen" because she never married. She forced all English to be members of the Church of England, imprisoning thousands and executing hundreds of Catholics. Her navy defeated the Spanish Armada in 1588.

5. King Louis XI: King Louis XI (ruled 1461-1483) was called "The Spider." Louis XI grew his empire by negotiation and treaties instead of war.

6. Valois Dynasty: From 1328 to 1589, the Valois Dynasty ruled France.

7. Charles VIII: Charles VIII (ruled Spain 1483-1498) was constantly at war with the Hapsburgs over northern Italy.

8. Francis I: Francis I (ruled France 1515-1547) gained the power of investiture. He was able to choose who became bishops and cardinals, and thus, controlled the Church.

9. Queen Isabella I of Castille and King Ferdinand II: Queen Isabella I of Castille and King Ferdinand II of Aragon (ruled Spain 1469-1516) founded the Spanish kingdom. It was a country of 11 million. They defeated the Moors. They expanded Spain by commissioning Christopher Columbus to sail, and he discovered America. After defeating the Muslims in 1492, they expelled all 150,000 Jews from Spain and created the Spanish Inquisition.

10. Charles I: Charles I (1516-1556) of the House of Habsburg became Holy Roman Emperor in 1519, joining the Kingdom of Spain with the Habsburg Empire. Charles I is the grandson of Queen Isabella I and King Ferdinand II.

37. Religious Wars and Kings' Wars

Europeans fought a series of devastating wars from 1550 to 1648. They began as religious wars of Catholic against Protestant but evolved into political wars of monarch against monarch. The Renaissance, the Reformation, a population rise, and the increase of power of the monarchs brought instability to the medieval order. Citizens' loyalty changed from God and the feudal lord to king and country.

King Phillip II of Spain (ruled 1556-1598) led the Catholics in fighting Protestantism and Islam in his Habsburg Empire of Spain, New Spain, northern Italy, and the Low Countries. Phillip II had success against the Muslims and failure against Protestants. At the **Battle of Lepanto** in 1571, the Habsburgs and a Christian coalition defended Europe against a Muslim invasion. In 1588, the English under **Queen Elizabeth I** (1533-1603) destroyed the world greatest fleet, the Spanish Armada, and saved Protestant England from invasion. Phillip II attempted to hold onto his colonies in northern Europe, but failed. Calvinist William of Orange led the revolt but was assassinated. In 1579, seven Dutch provinces broke from Spain and formed the **United Provinces**, later becoming the Netherlands.

In France, war raged between the Calvinists – called Huguenots – and Catholics. Atrocities happened on both sides, with the **Saint Bartholomew's Day Massacre** (1572) as perhaps the worst example. Beginning on the evening of a marriage between a royal Catholic and Protestant, Catholics murdered at least 2,000 Huguenots in Paris, and possibly up to 10,000 throughout France over the next weeks.

In England, **King Henry VIII and Queen Elizabeth I** waged war against Catholics, imprisoning thousands and executing hundreds. In Ireland, England abolished the **Gaelic language** and used starvation to try and exterminate the Catholic Irish. Historians estimate that over 30,000 Irish were killed in 1582.

The **Thirty Years War** (1618-1648) was fought in the Holy Roman Empire. What started as a religious war of Catholic versus Protestant became a political and economic war between kings. Originally, the Catholic Habsburgs fought the Protestant Bohemians, northern Germans, and Swedes. By 1631, Catholic France joined Protestant Gustavus Adolphus of Sweden and attacked the Catholic Holy Roman Empire. Catholic France and Spain then fought each other for European supremacy. French Prime Minister **Cardinal Richelieu** (1585-1642) was emblematic of the new politics of power. Europe became divided by kingdom instead of religion.

The **Treaty of Westphalia** (1648) ended the Thirty Years War. The peace treaty signaled the beginning of the modern era for Europe. Instead of just the major powers deciding the peace terms, all participants sent ambassadors. France and Sweden won territories and the United Provinces were recognized. The Habsburgs of the Holy Roman Empire lost power, as did the Pope, who refused to sign the treaty. France replaced Spain as Europe's main power. Never again did religion serve as the main source of loyalty for Europeans. In the war, more than 1/3 of Germans died, losing approximately 7 million people. One of three soldiers were killed. Disease was rampant. Trade stopped. Widespread destruction and total warfare (war against civilians) was the norm.

Facts to Know for Religious Wars and Kings' Wars

1. King Phillip II: King Phillip II of the Habsurg Dynasty (ruled 1556-1598) led the Catholics in fighting Protestantism and Islam. Phillip II had success against the Muslims and failure against Protestants.

2. Battle of Lepanto: At the Battle of Lepanto in 1571, the Habsburgs and a Christian coalition defended Europe against a Muslim invasion.

3. Queen Elizabeth I: Queen Elizabeth I (1533-1603) destroyed the world greatest fleet, the Spanish Armada, and saved Protestant England from Spanish invasion.

4. United Provinces: In 1579, seven Dutch provinces broke from Spain and formed the United Provinces, later becoming the Netherlands.

5. Saint Bartholomew's Day Massacre: Beginning on the evening of a marriage between a royal Catholic and Protestant, Catholics murdered at least 2,000 Huguenots in Paris in an event known as Saint Bartholomew's Day Massacre (1572).

6. King Henry VIII and Queen Elizabeth I: These two Tudor monarchs of the 1500s waged war against Catholics, imprisoning thousands and executing hundreds.

7. Thirty Years War: The Thirty Years War (1618-1648) was fought in the Holy Roman Empire. What started as a religious war of Catholic versus Protestant became a political and economic war of power between monarchs.

8. Cardinal Richelieu: French Prime Minister Cardinal Richelieu (1585-1642) was emblematic of the new politics

of power. Europe became divided by kingdom instead of religion.

9. Treaty of Westphalia: The Treaty of Westphalia (1648) ended the Thirty Years War. The peace treaty signaled the beginning of the modern era for Europe.

10. Gaelic language: The Gaelic language is the ancient language of the Irish. Queen Elizabeth I banned Gaelic and used starvation to try and exterminate the Catholic Irish. Historians estimate that over 30,000 Irish were killed in 1582.

38. Science, Inventions, and Medicine

In the 15th, 16th, and 17th centuries, Europeans changed the way they studied science. Scientists such as Rene Descartes, **Sir Francis Bacon**, and Galilei Galileo developed the use of the scientific method, a system of study that is aimed at reaching verifiable conclusions. A number of inventions during this time enabled scientists to make breakthroughs in the fields of astronomy, medicine, physics, chemistry, and navigation.

The scientific method is a process that scientists use to find natural explanations. These explanations help humans find solutions to diseases, enabled man to understand how the sun is the center of the universe, and can be used to make human life last longer.

Step one in the scientific method is to understand the problem. The scientist then makes a hypothesis, or guess, to explain it. The hypothesis is tested with an experiment that can be repeated. If the hypothesis does not resolve the problem, the scientist creates a new hypothesis and tests this with an experiment. If the hypothesis solves the problem, other scientists test the hypothesis. If the same results are reached, the hypothesis is accepted as a theory. A theory becomes a law if it is applicable universally.

New inventions like the telescope and the microscope enabled scientists to test theories of the natural world. The telescope is used to gaze at stars. It was invented in the Netherlands by eyeglass makers **Hans Lippershey and Hans Janssen** in the early 1600s. **Galileo** made great improvements of it and used it to formulate his heliocentric view of the world. Lippershey and Janssen also developed one of the first **microscopes**, used to investigate small objects. Galileo made improvements to their invention, as well.

The thermometer and barometer were developed during this time. Galileo was one of the scientists who worked on both of these, as well. The **thermometer** is used to measure the temperature of water or air, and the body. The **barometer** is used to measure the atmosphere by using water, air, or mercury and can predict short term weather.

Throughout the Medieval Ages, ancient Greeks dominated medicine. **Hippocrates** (460-377 B.C.) observed the human body and was a noted doctor. **Aristotle** (384-322 B.C.) wrote about the function of the parts of the body. **Galen** (A.D. 129-199) made observations of animals, performed experiments, and explained the parts of mammals.

Scientists of the Renaissance greatly improved medicine by use of the scientific method. Belgian **Andreas Vesalius** (1514-1564) was the first to dissect dead humans. He published a book on human anatomy, *On the Fabric of the Human Body*. He is the founder of modern human anatomy. Englishman **William Harvey** (1578-1657) explained the circulatory system in his book, *On the Motion of the Heart and Blood*. Before his work, it was thought blood flowed to and from the heart through the same vessels via a tidal system. Irish **Robert Boyle** (1627-1691) started modern chemistry.

Facts to Know for the Scientific Method, Inventions and Medicine

1. Sir Francis Bacon: Sir Francis Bacon (1561-1626) was an English philosopher who developed the Scientific Method.

2. Hans Lippershey and Hans Janssen: Hans Lippershey and Hans Janssen were eyeglass makers in the Netherlands who invented the telescope and developed one of the first microscopes in the 1600s.

3. Galilei Galileo: Galileo (1564-1642) was an Italian scientist who greatly improved the telescope and argued for a heliocentric understanding of the universe.

4. Microscope: This machine is used to observe small objects.

5. Thermometer: The thermometer is used to measure the temperature of water or air, and the body.

6. Barometer: The barometer is used to measure the atmosphere by using water, air, or mercury and can predict short term weather.

7. Hippocrates: The Greek Hippocrates (460-377 B.C.) observed the human body and was a noted doctor.

8. Aristotle: The Greek Aristotle (384-322 B.C.) wrote about the function of the parts of the body.

9. Galen: The Greek Galen (A.D. 129-199) made observations of animals, performed experiments, and explained the parts of mammals.

10. Andreas Vesalius: The Italian Andreas Vesalius (1514-1564) was the first to dissect dead humans. He published a book on human anatomy, *On the Fabric of the Human Body*. He is the founder of modern human anatomy.

11. William Harvey: Englishman William Harvey (1578-1657) explained the circulatory system in his book, *On the Motion of the Heart and Blood.*

12. Robert Boyle: Irish Robert Boyle (1627-1691) started modern chemistry.

39. Philosophy, Astronomy, Mathematics and Physics

For over 1,000 years, Europeans had relied on ancient Greek writings, the Catholic Church, and the Bible to explain how the natural world operated. In the 15th-17th centuries, all of this changed in what we call **The Scientific Revolution.** Instead of relying on the Church or Greek writings, all scientific ideas were put to the test of observation and experimentation. Frenchman **Rene Descartes** (1596-1690) was a mathematician who questioned the ability to have knowledge with absolute certainty. He wrote in *Discourse on Method* "I think, therefore I am", and posited that the only thing a person can know is his own existence. He was skeptical of any knowledge that dealt with the supernatural, like faith and religion.

Englishman **Sir Francis Bacon** (1561-1626) furthered this idea of relying on provable data to understand the world. In *Novum organum*, published in 1620, Bacon wrote that reason would help man form a more comfortable and better civilization. Through observation of much data, man could form general theories. Aristotle had written that man take general logical theories to explain the world.

Astronomy led the way in the Scientific Revolution. Polish priest and astronomer **Nicolaus Copernicus** (1473-1543) observed the orbit of the planets. Using mathematical calculations, he refuted **Ptolemy**'s understanding that the sun revolved around the earth. In *On the Revolutions of the Heavenly Bodies* he argued that the sun was the center of the universe. Danish astronomer **Tycho Brahe** (1576-1601) observed that the planets orbited in an elliptical, not circular, orbit. His assistant German **Johannes Kepler** (1571-1630) illustrated with a mathematical formula that Copernicus was correct.

Galilei Galileo (1564-1642) of Italy went beyond previous scientists by using observation and experimentation to prove verifiable conclusions. Until Galileo, scientists had argued their findings were theories. Using a telescope he improved from a Dutch lens crafter, Galileo confirmed Copernicus' theories about a heliocentric world. Galileo came into conflict with Catholic Church authorities. His *Dialogue on the Two Chief Systems of the World* (1632), showed that only a simpleton could believe in a geocentric world. He wrote that the Bible supported his findings. The Church supported a geocentric viewpoint of the world and forbade most from interpreting Scripture. It wanted Galileo to say his conclusions were theories. He refused. Galileo was placed under house arrest but was allowed to continue his work.

Englishman **Sir Isaac Newton** (1642-1727) brought together the theories of Copernicus and Kepler and the observations of Galileo to formulate laws governing falling bodies. Newton was a strong Christian and rejected Desacartes' view that religion and faith were false. In *Mathematical Principles of Natural Philosophy*, published in 1687, he presented three laws to describe how the universe worked:

> 1. Motion continues in a straight line without force,
> 2. The rate of change of motion is determined by the forces acting on it, and
> 3. Action and reaction between two bodies are equal and opposite.

Facts to Know for Philosophy, Astronomy, Mathematics and Physics

1. The Scientific Revolution: In the 15th-17th centuries, instead of relying on the Church or Greek writings, all scientific ideas were put to the test of observation and experimentation in the Scientific Revolution.

2. Rene Descartes: Frenchman Rene Descartes (1596-1690) was a mathematician who questioned the ability to have knowledge with absolute certainty.

3. Sir Francis Bacon: Sir Francis Bacon (1561-1626) wrote about using observation and experimentation to understand the world.

4. Nicolaus Copernicus: Polish priest Nicolaus Copernicus (1473-1543) observed the orbit of the planets. Using mathematical calculations, he refuted Ptolemy's understanding that the sun revolved around the earth and wrote that the earth revolved around the sun.

5. Ptolemy: Ptolemy was an ancient Greek who wrote the sun revolved around the earth.

6. Tycho Brahe: Danish astronomer Tycho Brahe (1576-1601) observed that the planets orbited in an elliptical, not circular, orbit.

7. Johannes Kepler: German Johannes Kepler (1571-1630) illustrated with a mathematical formula that Copernicus was correct.

8. Galilei Galileo: Galilei Galileo (1564-1642) of Italy went beyond previous scientists by using observation and experimentation to prove verifiable conclusions.

9. Sir Isaac Newton: Englishman Sir Isaac Newton (1642-1727) brought together the theories of Copernicus and Kepler and the observations of Galileo to formulate laws governing falling bodies.

10. *Mathematical Principles of Natural Philosophy*: Isaac Newton, in *Mathematical Principles of Natural Philosophy*, published in 1687, presented three laws to describe how the universe worked:
>1. Motion continues in a straight line without force,
>2. The rate of change of motion is determined by the forces acting on it, and
>3. Action and reaction between two bodies are equal and opposite.

40. The Age of Absolutism

After **Treaty of Westphalia** (1648) strong central governments emerged and monarchs took absolute control over the government and people. High taxation, standing armies and large bureaucracies held subjects under tight control. Kings promoted the idea that the monarch was absolute and that his power came from God. The **divine right of kings** meant that God chose the king to be ruler and all had to obey. Kings were anointed at coronation with holy oils and received blessing from god, like a sacrament.

Nowhere else was absolutism best exhibited than in France with the Valois Dynasty. **King Louis XIV** (ruled 1643-1715) was called the "Sun King," as if rays of sunlight came from him. Louis kept a permanent army and built a huge palace, Versailles, where he forced all nobles to live next to him. At **Versailles**, King Louis XIV enforced rules of etiquette meant to make everyone obey the king and to focus on fashion. Nobles were not allowed to wear the same clothing two days in a row. France fought many wars, such as the War against the United Provinces (1672-1678), war against Spain, and against England. King Louis XIV forced all French to worship as Catholics or leave the country.

The **Habsburg Dynasty**, centered in Vienna, also exhibited an absolute monarch. King Leopold I was also Holy Roman Emperor (ruled 1685-1705). He emulated King Louis XIV and made the palace at Schonbrunn in Vienna his "Versailles." Emperor Leopold I loved music, was a composer, and he turned Vienna into a music center of the world. Under the Habsburgs, Prince Eugene defended Europe and the Holy Roman Empire from the Turks. **Maria Theresa** (ruled 1740-1780) inherited an empire that was poorer than Prussia, but she transformed the Habsburg

Empire into perhaps the strongest in central Europe. Maria had 16 children and enforced Catholicism in the empire. She reformed the education and military system to create a strong government.

In the north of Europe was **Prussia**, with its capital in Berlin. Prince Frederick William I (ruled 1713-1740) of Hohenzollern expanded his power and made the Prussian army perhaps the most formidable in Europe. Everything in the state was geared to serve the state and the army, including education. Prussia enforced compulsory education, so students would learn how to serve the state. Every Prussian had to be Lutheran. Frederick II (ruled 1740-1786) was raised by his father to be tough, a soldier, and to be aggressive. Frederick II conquered Silesia from the Habsburgs and is known as **Frederick the Great.**

In Russia, Tsar Peter I (ruled 1682-1725), called **Peter the Great**, consolidated his power, took over the Eastern Orthodox Church, and subjugated all to the **Tsar** (In Russia, people called their leader this. It is short for Caesar, or, Emperor). Peter had the city of Saint Petersburg built in his honor. During the building, thousands of serfs died. As a young man, Peter disguised himself and lived in other countries. He returned to Russia, bringing European ideas and people to his court to modernize his own country. He created three classes in society. All peasants were forced into conscription and had to perform public works. Below them were serfs, who were outlawed to move. His upper class was the bureaucracy, where only the aristocracy could hold an office. He conferred new titles and land and serfs to the nobles, who were forced to build mansions in St Petersburg and to hold public offices.

Facts to Know for The Age of Absolutism

1. The Treaty of Westphalia: The Treaty of Westphalia (1648) established the modern countries and boundaries of Europe and signaled the beginning of the Age of Absolutism.

2. Divine Right of Kings: The divine right of kings meant that God chose the king to be ruler and all had to obey.

3. King Louis XIV: King Louis XIV (ruled 1643-1715) ruled France as an absolute monarch, built a strong army, built the huge palace at Versailles, and controlled his nobles and subjects.

4. Versailles: At Versailles, King Louis XIV enforced rules of etiquette meant to make everyone obey the king and to focus on fashion. Nobles were not allowed to wear the same clothing two days in a row.

5. Habsburg Dynasty: The Habsburg Dynasty, centered in Vienna, built Vienna into the music capital of the world, defended the Turks from conquering Europe, and created a modern bureaucratic state.

6. Maria Theresa: Maria Theresa (ruled 1740-1780) inherited an empire that was poorer than Prussia, but she transformed the Habsburg Empire into perhaps the strongest in central Europe.

7. Prussia: Located in northern Europe, Prussia became perhaps the strongest military state.

8. Frederick II: Frederick II conquered Silesia from the Habsburgs and is known as Frederick the Great.

9. Peter the Great: In Russia, Tsar Peter I (ruled 1682-1725), called Peter the Great, consolidated his power, took over the Eastern Orthodox Church, and subjugated all.

10. Tsar: In Russia, people called their leader this. It is short for Caesar, or, Emperor).

41. The Age of Revolution, 1776-1848

From **1776-1848**, citizens in different continents rose up against their governments and tried to overthrow them. In all cases, the story was similar. Leaders felt protected by centuries of tradition that gave an elite ruling class more rights than average citizens. Citizens realized the current condition was unjust, and so they tried to change not only who led the country but how the government was organized. In some cases, the revolutionaries were successful. In other cases, the revolution caused a backlash against the revolutionaries and an even more strict and dominant ruling elite emerged.

The **American Revolution**, 1775-1783, was the first of many revolutions during this time period. In this case, English colonists in America protested against the rule of **King George III** and the English Parliament. Colonists wanted the right to choose their own leaders and did not want to pay taxes to the British unless colonists voted for the taxes. King George III tried to hike taxes, regulate the economy, control the colonists with soldiers, and appoint Royal Governors. Colonists declared themselves independent with the **Declaration of Independence**, raised an army, and defeated the strongest country on earth, Great Britain. American patriots wrote the Constitution and established the freest country on earth.

In France, French revolutionaries attempted to overthrow the system of monarchy and replace it with something more democratic. In **1789**, citizens overthrew King Louis XVI, decapitating him, and believed they were on the way toward "liberty, equality, and fraternity." However, the revolution got out of control. Revolutionaries were not happy with getting rid of the king, and saw everywhere "enemies of the state." Innocent French citizens were killed, Catholic priests were tortured and executed, and chaos reigned. In 1799, Napoleon Bonaparte took over as a military commander and in 1804 declared himself "Emperor Napoleon."

From 1804-1829, **Latin American Revolutionaries** revolted and took down their Spanish, Portuguese, and French colonizers. In nearly all of the new countries that emerged, revolutionaries tried to establish a democratic republic as existed in the United States of America. The newly-formed countries of Venezuela, Columbia, Brazil, Peru, Ecuador, Uruguay, Paraguay, Chile, Bolivia, Haiti, and Mexico all descended into chaos and anarchy, and eventually, military dictatorships.

In **1848,** across Europe, revolutionaries demanded democratic changes to the monarchies that ruled them. In France, Prussia, Austro-Hungary, and Italy, rebels rose up through writing articles, giving speeches, and eventually, taking up arms against the armies. In the end, the "Old Guard" of Europe prevailed. It wasn't until after World War I that many Europeans gained the right to vote.

Facts to Know for The Age of Revolution, 1776-1848

1. The Age of Revolution, 1776-1848: In this time period, citizens in different continents rose up against their governments and tried to overthrow them.

2. The American Revolution, 1775-1783: English colonists defeated Great Britain, establishing a constitutional republic and the new country, the United States of America.

3. King George III: King George III ruled Great Britain during the American Revolution.

4. The Declaration of Independence: Thomas Jefferson authored the Declaration of Independence and the Continental Congress approved on July 4, 1776. This declared the United States of America is a new country.

5. The French Revolution, 1789: In 1789, the French Revolution began. Revolutionaries executed French King XVI and tried to establish a more democratic country. Bonaparte, instead, established an empire ruled by one person.

6. Latin American Revolutions, 1804-1829: Latin American revolutionaries overthrew their European colonizers and attempted to establish democratic republics. Instead, military dictatorships took control of the new countries.

7. 1848 Revolutions: In 1848 across Europe, revolutionaries attempted but failed to overthrow their governments and establish democratic countries.

42. Industrial Revolution

European "**Enlightenment**" thinkers believed in liberty, equality, republican government, property rights, and science. These beliefs had huge economic effects. Rational enlightened men could use scientific method to invent new products, market them, and grow wealthy. The industrial revolution of the late 1700s and 1800s was fueled by this inventive spirit. In nations that protected **property rights**, inventors, industrialists, and workers were motivated to produce wealth. This marked the beginning of an economic system called **capitalism**.

Beginning in the 1760s, England became the first nation to industrialize. Englishmen had all the elements necessary for **industrialization**: capital (investors), labor, raw materials, innovative technology, transportation, markets, and a government that protected private property rights. Between 1760 and 1860, personal income among England's poorest workers rose 70%. But in the short run, industrial efficiency cost many folks like small farmers their jobs and forced them to learn new skills to earn a living.

Scotsman **Adam Smith** was a founder of free market-- "**classical liberal**"--economic thought. Smith believed men could accomplish great ends if the government left them free to do so. In 1776, he published *An Inquiry Into the Natures and Causes of the Wealth of Nations*. Smith argued that all business transactions were governed by the "**invisible hand**" of competition, supply and demand, and man's rational self-interest. He stated that government should leave the economy alone, allowing market forces to create wealth and prosperity.

In industrializing nations in the 1800s, the work force was made up of ex-farmers, women and children, and in America, foreign immigrants. This generation of workers was forced to learn new skills and labor long hours before returning home to poor and unhealthy neighborhoods. Nevertheless, workers found their new jobs offered them opportunities. Between **1840 and 1900**, British workers' wages doubled, life expectancy rose by 20%, and there were marked improvements in nutrition, health, and school attendance.

Facts to Know for the Industrial Revolution

1. Enlightenment: This was an intellectual movement in 17th and 18th century European thinkers who believed in liberty, equality, republican government, property rights, and science.

2. Property Rights: This means that individuals have the right to own private property, and their property is protected by the government.

3. Capitalism: This means an economic "system" where individuals have freedom how to earn money, how to spend what they earn, and how to make choices involving their economic life. Another way of saying this is the free market.

4. Industrialization: This means when a society moves from making everything by hand and individually to producing things in factories, in larger scales, and by using technology to power factories.

5. Adam Smith: This 18th century English author described the system of the free market in his writings.

6. Classical Liberal: This means when an individual believes it is best when the government does as little as possible, so that individuals have freedom at act, to think, to speak, to own private property, and to be in charge of their own lives.

7. Invisible Hand: Adam Smith explained that the economy in a free market is run by an "invisible hand," which is the relationship of supply and demand and how individuals choose what is valuable and what is not.

43. Peace, Free Trade, and Liberalism

Great Britain's and Prussia's 1815 military triumph over French Emperor Napoleon Bonaparte completely transformed European and global politics. European monarchs called a great meeting in Vienna in 1815 to plan a new world power structure. Under the leadership of Austria's Prince Metternich, Britain, Prussia, and Russia dismantled Napoleon's empire and redrew Europe's boundaries with the goal of halting democracy and establishing "**balance of power**" between themselves. With a few exceptions, the **Treaty of Vienna** created a stable and peaceful Europe for a century.

During 700 years of warfare, Britain and France attacked one another's ships and those of any nation they suspected of trading with their enemy. This militant regulation of trade was part of a European economic system called "**mercantilism**." The 1815 defeat of Napoleon and subsequent Congress of Vienna treaty marked the retreat of mercantilism and beginning of "**Freedom of the Seas**." With some exceptions, the 1800s was a time of freer markets and freer trade for European nations and the United States of America.

The fledging U.S. republic benefitted immensely from the peace and stability that followed Napoleon's defeat. With Britain and France no longer at war, Americans could at last enjoy freedom of the seas and assert their new independence. As America's global trade blossomed, U.S. President James Monroe announced the **Monroe Doctrine** stating the United States would stay out of European diplomatic and military affairs so long as European powers did not meddle in the affairs of the U.S. and the new Latin American republics.

The early Enlightenment ideas of John Locke and Adam Smith flowered in the 1800s in a political and economic philosophy called "**classical liberalism**." Classical liberals like **John Stuart Mill** believed property rights were the basis of all liberties. They advocated peace, an unregulated "free market" economy, freedom of religion and speech, and a balanced, representative government based on a constitution and statute law. Classical liberals believed the only duty of government was to protect citizens' lives, liberty, and property.

Facts to Know for Peace, Free Trade, and Liberalism

1. Balance of Power: This term means when the countries of Europe allied themselves so that one country or one side would never have too much power over the other side. This balance of power made no country threatened and was good for peace.

2. Treaty of Vienna, 1815: This treaty was between the major European powers. These countries agreed to maintain the monarchy and to abide by a balance of power within Europe.

3. Mercantilism: This was an economic system where each European country tried to gain as many natural resources as possible for the king. Countries would attack other countries at sea to destroy the trading power of others.

4. Freedom of the Seas: This was a policy put in place after the Treaty of Vienna which ensured that countries could trade at sea without the threat of having their ships and sailors attacked.

5. The Monroe Doctrine, 1820: James Monroe established this policy of the United States of America that no outside power would play an important or military role in the affairs of countries of North and South America.

6. Classical Liberalism: This policy argued that property rights were the basis of all liberties. It advocated peace, an unregulated "free market" economy, freedom of religion and speech, and a balanced, representative government based on a constitution and statute law.

7. John Stuart Mill: Mill was an English Member of Parliament and strong proponent of classical liberalism.

44. British Colonialism

Nineteenth century European nations practiced **colonialism**--conquering weaker people in undeveloped lands to achieve economic, military, religious, scientific, and social goals. Great Britain took **Australia** from aboriginal people and used it as a penal colony. Beginning in 1788, Britons shipped convicted criminals from London's crowded jails to Botany Bay (Sydney) and across Australia. By the time the system ended in 1868, 164,000 men and women had been transported and jailed. Their descendants make up an estimated 20% of the population of modern Australia.

Canadian and American histories show there were vast differences within Britain's North American colonial system. The British took **Canada and America** from native Indians for economic, military, scientific, social, and religious reasons. British-American colonists resisted royal authority, launched the American Revolution in 1776, and established an independent republic. On the other hand, Canadians never revolted from British rule. Very slowly, Anglo- and French-Canadians gained autonomy through Britain's 1867 British North America Act, the 1931 Statute of Westminster, and, finally, the 1982 Canada Act.

Native people resisted British colonialism. The **British East India Company,** a government sub-contractor, first colonized India in 1608. Opposition slowly arose among native Indians who demanded self-rule. The famed 1857-59 "**Indian Mutiny**" was the first organized Indian rebellion against British rule. Native Sepoy troops serving the East India Company attacked their British overlords. Although they met defeat, their revolt became known among Indians as the First War of Independence. The **Indian Independence Act of 1947** granted autonomy to both India and Pakistan.

Both native South Africans and Dutch colonists resisted British colonialism. The Dutch settled Capetown in 1652 and the British arrived much later in 1806. To escape British rule, Dutch "Boers" (farmers) trekked north across the mountains where they settled and adopted elements of African herding culture, calling themselves "**Afrikaners**." Although they lost the Boer Wars (1880-81 and 1899-1902) to Britain, Afrikaners achieved independence and segregated native people in a racist "**apartheid**" system. Native South Africans won their own independence in 1994.

Facts to Know for British Colonialism

1. colonialism: This is the act of conquering weaker people in undeveloped lands to achieve economic, military, religious, scientific, and social goals.

2. Australia: Great Britain took this land from aboriginal people and used it as a penal colony.

3. Canada and America: British took land from native Indians for economic, military, scientific, social, and religious reasons. Canadians never revolted but gained independence over the centuries. The American revolted and established an independent country in 1776.

4. The British East India Company: This was the government sub-contractor, which first colonized India in 1608.

5. Indian Mutiny, 1857-1859: This was the first organized Indian rebellion against British rule.

6. The Indian Independence Act of 1947: This granted autonomy to both India and Pakistan.

7. Afrikaners: These were Dutch settlers who trekked across the mountains and established a separate country from the British in South Africa.

8. Apartheid: Afrikaners established a racist country, the Republic of South Africa, that placed Blacks as second-class citizens with minimal rights.

45. The Radical Left

The political labeling of **the "Left"** began during the French Revolution because the most radical Frenchmen sat on the left side of the Estates General (legislature). As the Revolution progressed, a group calling themselves **"Jacobins"** arose as violent advocates of democracy and social equality. Led by Maximilien Robespierre in 1792-94, Jacobins beheaded King Louis XVI and waged a **"Reign of Terror,"** murdering aristocrats and Catholic priests. But Jacobin anarchy soon produced dictatorship--by 1799, Napoleon Bonaparte ruled France.

German **Karl Marx** helped found the **Communist** movement. Communists believed citizens do not have a right to private property and the government should own all the means of economic production. In 1848, Marx and his collaborator **Friedrich Engels** wrote *The Communist Manifesto*. The *Manifesto* advocated a heavy income tax, abolition of inheritance, confiscation of property, free public education, abolition of child labor, a national bank, national transportation and communication systems, and redistribution of population to create industrial and agricultural "armies."

During the "**Revolutions of 1848**," protestors across France, Austria, Germany, and Italy unsuccessfully strove to replace monarchy and hierarchy with democracy, social equality, and nationalism. While most revolutionaries were liberals who believed in property rights, some were radical socialists and Communists. Radicals flew red flags symbolizing the blood of the working class, and Karl Marx and Friedrich Engels published *The Communist Manifesto*. Although a minor faction in 1848, Communists represented the future of the radical Left in Europe.

Twentieth century Marxist revolutionaries overthrew autocratic monarchs and replaced them with communist dictators. In Russia, leftists murdered **Czar Nicholas II** in 1917. By 1927 they had seized all private property and established the **Union of Soviet Socialist Republics** ruled by **Joseph Stalin**. Chinese republicans overthrew the Qing Dynasty in 1911. But communists and nationalists fought a civil war from 1927-49, ending in the communist dictatorship of **Mao Zedong.** During the twentieth century, Russian and Chinese communists retained power by murdering, imprisoning, and torturing tens of millions of their own citizens.

Facts to Know for The Radical Left

1. The Left: This refers to the people who want to redistribute wealth in society, regardless of who creates or owns the wealth. The radical left wants to control all property and means of production and thinks the individual should be obedient to the state. In the 20th century, the radical left tortured and murdered tens of millions, some say 100 million, of innocent people.

2. Jacobins: These were violent proponents of radical change in France during the French Revolution. They were responsible for the murder of tens of thousands of innocent people.

3. Reign of Terror, 1792-1794: During the French Revolution, the Jacobins murdered tens of thousands of people to try to implement what they saw as the perfect society.

4. Karl Marx and Frederich Engels: These two were the founders of the modern Communist movement.

5. Communists: These people believe citizens do not have a right to private property and the government should own all the means of economic production.

6. The Communist Manifesto: The *Manifesto* advocated a heavy income tax, abolition of inheritance, confiscation of property, free public education, abolition of child labor, a national bank, national transportation and communication systems, and redistribution of population to create industrial and agricultural "armies." It supported using terror and violence to achieve its ends.

7. Revolutions of 1848: Protestors across France, Austria, Germany, and Italy unsuccessfully strove to replace

monarchy and hierarchy with democracy, social equality, and nationalism.

8. Czar Nicholas II: He was the last Czar of Russia. Communists murdered him and his family in 1917.

9. Union of Soviet Socialist Republics (USSR): Communists established this country in 1922.

10. Joseph Stalin: He was the Communist leader of the USSR from 1922 to 1953 and was responsible for the murder from 25 to 40 million Soviets.

11. Mao Zedong: He was the Communist leader of China from 1949-1976 and was responsible for the murder from 40 to 80 million Chinese.

46. Nationalism and Unification

Germany was one of the last regions in Europe to become a modern "**nation state**." With some exceptions, nation states are strong, centralized governmental units in which most citizens are united by their culture--language, religion, ethnicity, principles, and patriotism. Prince **Otto Von Bismarck**, a Prussian leader and diplomat, played a crucial role in uniting the multiple German kingdoms of the old Holy Roman Empire under Prussian King **("Kaiser") Wilhelm I** in 1871. United Germany became a major European power.

For centuries, the Italian peninsula was divided into numerous city states and kingdoms. During the revolutionary ferment of the 1830s and 1840s, nationalist **Giuseppe Mazzini**'s movement to unify Italy steadily gathered followers. An army led by the famed patriot Giuseppe Garibaldi conquered Sicily and Naples in 1860. They joined Sardinia-Piedmont and northern Italian kingdoms in 1861 to form the Kingdom of Italy led by Sardinian Monarch **Emanuel II**. By 1871, Venezia and Rome had both joined and Italy took its place among modern European nation states.

Japanese people shared a common ethnicity, language, religion, and culture, but it was not until the late 1800s that they gained the strong government, military, and patriotic loyalty necessary to become a nation state. From 1600-1868, **Tokugawa Shoguns** centralized and stabilized the kingdom. Meiji leaders who followed in the late 1800s introduced a constitutional government under the emperor, parliament, and a prime minister. The new Japanese government fostered patriotism, resisted Western colonization, and established Japan as a world power.

In 1911, China's government transitioned from absolute monarchy to republican nation state. **Sun Yat-sen** (1866-

1925) led the movement that ended 2000 years of rule by all-powerful Emperors. As the Republic of China's first President, he battled warlords and negotiated a fragile truce between his Chinese Nationalist Party ("Kuomintang") and **Mao Zedong**'s Chinese Communists. In 1949, Mao's army defeated Nationalist **Chiang Kai-shek**'s forces. Mao became leader of the People's Republic of China while Chiang led the Nationalist Chinese on the island of Taiwan.

Facts to Know for Nationalism and Unification

1. Nation State: With some exceptions, nation states are strong, centralized governmental units in which most citizens are united by their culture--language, religion, ethnicity, principles, and patriotism.

2. Otto Von Bismarck: He was a Prussian leader and diplomat and played a crucial role in uniting the multiple German kingdoms of the old Holy Roman Empire.

3. King ("Kaiser") Wilhelm I: He was a Prussian leader who became the first German King.

4. Giuseppe Mazzini: He was an Italian nationalist who worked towards a unified Italian kingdom.

5. Emmanuel II: He became Italy's first king.

6. Tokugawa Shoguns: They centralized and stabilized the kingdom of Japan.

7. Sun Yat-sen: He led the movement that ended 2000 years of rule by all-powerful Emperors. As the Republic of China's first President, he battled warlords and negotiated a fragile truce between his Chinese Nationalist Party ("Kuomintang") and Mao Zedong's Chinese Communists.

8. Mao Zedong: Mao was leader of the Communist People's Republic of China from 1949-1976.

9. Chang Kai-Shek: He became the leader of Taiwan.

47. World War I

World War I (1914-1918) broke out in Europe in 1914 due to entangling alliances within the British, French, and Russian alliance system and that of the Central Powers--Germany, Austria-Hungary, and Turkey. World War I marked the beginning of "**Total War**," meaning airplanes, machine guns, tanks, submarines, poison gas, and civilian casualties. America entered World War I in 1917 on the side of Britain, France, and Russia, and U.S. forces tipped the scales to score an Allied victory.

During World War I, Britain and France fought Germany to a stalemate along the "**Western Front**" in Belgium and northern France. Millions of opposing troops lived for months in long trenches and fortifications; they recurrently crossed the "No Man's Land" separating them to attack the enemy to no avail. All the horrors of modern warfare combined with disease to ultimately kill 8,500,000 men. German soldier **Erich Maria Remarque**'s 1929 novel *All Quiet on the Western Front* described the horrors of trench warfare.

The 1919 **Treaty of Versailles** ending World War I was signed by defeated Germany and its Allied foes Britain, France, and the United States. Although the Treaty created a **League of Nations** to discuss world problems, the United States never joined the League. The Treaty stripped Germany of many territorial possessions and imposed huge "**war reparations**" payments that the indebted Germans had to pay the victorious Allies. In fact, the vengeful Treaty of Versailles set the stage for World War II.

Although the 1920s decade following World War I initially brought economic gains to the United States and other Allied victors, within a generation there was a world-wide **Depression**. Germans, saddled with enormous "reparations" payments to the Allies, suffered greatly;

German currency became so inflated and worthless that some folks used it to kindle fires. European economic collapse also brought tyranny as Germans, Italians, and Spaniards were drawn to the charismatic Nazi and fascist socialists Adolf Hitler, Benito Mussolini, and Francisco Franco.

Facts to Know for World War I

1. World War I: Lasting from 1914-1918, this war was between British, French, and Russian alliance system (The Allies) and that of the Central Powers--Germany, Austria-Hungary, and Turkey. The United States of America joined the Allies in 1917.

2. Total War: This meant airplanes, machine guns, tanks, submarines, poison gas, and civilian casualties. The entire population played a role in fighting the war.

3. Western Front: In the West, France and Great Britain fought Germany to a stalemate in Belgium and France.

4. Erich Maria Remarque: This German soldier's book, *All Quiet on the Western Front,* describes the horrors of the war.

5. Treaty of Versailles, 1919: This treaty ended the war and placed great blame against Germany. Germany was forced to give up land and to pay war reparations to the victorious countries.

6. League of Nations: The Treaty of Versailles created a worldwide association where world problems were discussed as a means to avoid war.

7. War Reparations: These were payments that the indebted Germans had to pay the victorious Allies.

8. Depression: This means a massive economic downturn that affects all of society.

48. Totalitarianism

During the 1920s and 1930s, totalitarian governments took power in Germany, Spain, Italy, Russia, and Japan. Some were ruled by "fascist" military tyrants who opposed democracy and espoused racism, seizure of other nations' lands, and socialism. Some were ruled by atheist Communists who opposed democracy, the free market, traditional morals, religion, and who sought absolute power over the individuals in a society. They are called **totalitarian** because these governments sought total power over the state and the individual.

German Karl Marx' *Communist Manifesto* inspired revolutionaries around the globe, including Russia. **Communists** are atheists who do not believe in democracy or private property. They advocate government control of all means of economic production. Twentieth century Marxist revolutionaries successfully overthrew autocratic monarchs and replaced them with communist dictatorships. In Russia, leftists murdered Czar Nicholas II in 1917 and by 1927 had seized all private property and murdered millions of citizens to establish Joseph Stalin as dictator of the **Union of Soviet Socialist Republics**.

Although China's government briefly transitioned from absolute monarchy to republican nation state in the early twentieth century, authoritarianism soon returned. Soon after Sun Yat-sen's followers ended 2000 years of rule by all-powerful Emperors, his Chinese Nationalist Party ("Kuomintang") was challenged and **Mao Zedong's** Chinese Communist Party. In 1949, Mao's army defeated Nationalist Chiang Kai-shek's forces and Mao became dictator of the People's Republic of China. Mao abolished private property and purged his political rivals.

German fascists formed the **Nazi Party** in 1920 in the wake of their World War I defeat, and the Nazis grew steadily as Germany's economic crisis worsened. In 1933, Nazi leader **Adolf Hitler** gained power in Germany in 1933 and worked steadily to annex adjacent territories and persecute the Jews.

In the late 1800s, **Meiji leaders** brought the Japanese people the strong military, constitutional government, and patriotic loyalty necessary to become a modern nation state. However, the Japanese lacked experience in representative democracy and by the 1920s and 30s a small group of military officers exercised great influence over the Emperor, Prime Minister, and Parliament. Suffering from the economic Depression, Japan soon embarked on a course of militaristic expansion, invading China and threatening the nations of south-east Asia and the Pacific Islands.

Facts to Know for Totalitarianism

1. Totalitarian: Governments are called this when they seek total power over the state and the individual.

2. Communists: These are atheists who do not believe in democracy or private property. They advocate government control of all means of economic production.

3. Union of Soviet Socialist Republics: This Communist country seized all private property, killed or jailed religious leaders, murdered the former leader and his family, and sought total control over the population. Terror and murder were used on a large scale from 1922 until its fall in 1991.

4. Mao Zedong: This Communist leader took total control over China in 1949 and was responsible with the Chinese Communist Party for the torture and murder of tens of millions of people.

5. Nazi Party: This name stands for the National Socialist German Workers Party. It seized power in Germany in the 1930s and was responsible for the murder of 11 million people, 6 million of them Jews, and for starting and conducting World War II.

6. Adolf Hitler: He was leader of the Nazi Party and responsible for everything the Nazi Party did.

7. Meiji Leaders: These Japanese leaders took over power from the emperor and parliament and embarked on military expansion that ultimately led to World War II in the Pacific.

49. World War II

As a result of chaos and economic depression following World War I, totalitarians took power in Germany, Spain, Italy, and Japan. These **"fascists"** preached racism, socialism, and seizure of other nations' lands. As German and Japanese forces began to invade and occupy bordering nations in the 1930s, western democracies joined the **totalitarian communist Soviet Union** to oppose them. By 1941, World War II pitted the **"Axis"** coalition of Germany, Italy, and Japan against the **"Allies"** Britain, France, the **Soviet Union**, United States, and Nationalist China.

World War II (1939-45) was a global conflict pitting "Allies" against the fascist "Axis" powers. There were two "theaters" of war. In Europe, Allies attacked by way of Italy and western France with the goal of capturing Berlin while Soviets attacked Germany from the east. In the Pacific, the Chinese battled Japan while their American allies fought across the Pacific Islands moving towards Tokyo. **"VE Day"**—Victory in Europe Day—came on May 8, 1945 while **"VJ Day"** marked Japan's September 2, 1945 surrender.

Nazi German leader **Adolph Hitler** was a racist who despised Jews, Slavs, blacks, and other minorities. Hitler proposed a "Final Solution" for "Mongrel Races" through **genocide**—the intentional act of destroying a people in whole or part. In German concentration camps, victorious American troops found incinerators, gas chambers, and thousands of dead bodies. The Nazis had murdered 10,000,000 innocent civilians, including 6,000,000 Jews. Soon after the war, the United Nations created the state of Israel as a homeland for Jews who survived this **"Holocaust."**

Although 400,000 American soldiers died in World War II, the toll could have been much higher. The Japanese ferociously opposed U.S. forces advancing across the Pacific islands and often chose suicide over surrender. By the summer of 1945, **President Harry S. Truman** decided to avoid further American deaths by dropping the newly invented **Atom Bomb** on the Japanese cities of Hiroshima and Nagasaki. Over 200,000 civilians died, Japan surrendered, and World War II immediately ended. No nation has since dared to use this powerful weapon.

Facts to Know for World War II

1. Fascists: The governments of Germany, Italy, Spain, and Japan could be described as fascist. They preached racism, socialism, and seizure of other nations' lands.

2. Axis: This was the coalition of Germany, Japan, and Italy in World War II.

3. Allies: This was the coalition of the United States of America, Great Britain, France, and the Soviet Union in World War II.

4. Totalitarian Communist Soviet Union: The Soviet Union's government was totalitarian and communist. It sought to totally control its population, owned all property, made all economic decisions, outlawed religion, and used terror and violence to control its people.

5. World War II (1939-1945): This was a global war of Allies versus Axis countries. It had two theaters of war: the West in Europe and Africa and the East in Asia.

6. VE Day: Victory in Europe Day came on May 8, 1945.

7. VJ Day: Victory in Japan Day came on September 2nd, 1945.

8. President Harry S. Truman: He became the U.S. President towards the end of the war.

9. Atom Bomb: In order to end the war the fastest way with the least amount of casualties, President Truman decided to drop the atom bomb on Nagasaki and Hiroshima. Over 200,000 Japanese were killed or wounded.

50. Rise and Fall of Communism

Because **20,000,000 Soviets died** in World War II, dictator Joseph Stalin vowed to never allow Germany to attack the Soviet Union again. To create a **buffer zone,** Soviet armies permanently occupied Poland, Czechoslovakia, Hungary, Yugoslavia, Romania, and other eastern European nations in 1945. The Soviets forced these nations to become "**satellites**"--communist regimes under control of Moscow. Western democracies were alarmed at this aggression and England's **Winston Churchill** declared, "an **iron curtain** has descended across the Continent." **The Cold War** had begun.

From 1910-45, Japan occupied the Korean peninsula of east Asia. With Japanese defeat in World War II, Soviet troops marched into North Korea but halted at the **38th parallel**, garrisoned by U.S. soldiers. The **Korean War** broke out in 1950 between the armies of communist North Korean dictator **Kim Il-sung** and South Korea's President Syngman Rhee. U.S. President Harry Truman persuaded the United Nations to support American and South Korean troops while Soviet and Chinese communists aided the North. The Korean War ended in stalemate in 1953.

The southeast Asian nation of Vietnam was a French colony seized by Japan in 1940. The French tried to regain control following Japan's defeat in World War II, but Vietnamese communist **Ho Chi Minh**'s army defeated them in 1954. Vietnam was divided at the 17th parallel and America replaced France as South Vietnam's ally against Ho's communist North. America fought its own **Vietnam War** to a 1963-1973 stalemate and withdrew. By 1975, communist North Vietnam conquered the south and a bloodbath of retribution followed.

The "Cold War" between communist nations and the United States lasted from approximately 1947-1991. It slowly became apparent to communists that no nation could prosper without property rights and human liberties. In 1987, U.S. President **Ronald Reagan** visited the vast concrete wall separating downtrodden communist East Berlin from West Berlin, its prosperous democratic neighbor. In a stirring speech, Reagan challenged Soviet leader Mikhail Gorbachev: **"Mr. Gorbachev, tear down this wall!"** The **Berlin Wall**, along with Soviet and European communism, dissolved in 1991.

Facts to Know for Rise and Fall of Communism

1. 20,000,000 Soviets Die: In World War II, 20 million Soviets were killed.

2. Buffer Zone: Soviet leader Stalin wanted to create a buffer zone in between the Soviet Union and Germany to protect the U.S.S.R. Soviet armies occupied Poland, Czechoslovakia, Hungary, Yugoslavia, Romania, and other eastern European nations.

3. Satellites: There were communist regimes under control of Moscow (the Soviet Union).

4. Winston Churchill: He was the Prime Minister of Great Britain during and after World War II.

5. Iron Curtain: Churchill announced that the Soviet Union controlled the Eastern European countries and created a metaphorical iron wall between the free countries of the West and the communist-controlled countries of the East.

6. The Cold War: This lasted from 1947-1991 and pitted the Communist Soviet Union against the Constitutional Republic United States of America. The two countries never fought each other directly in war, but battled each other through other countries and in every area. It ended with the defeat of the Communist Soviet Union.

7. 38th Parallel: This is the demarcation between communist North Korea and free South Korea.

8. The Korean War: In 1950, North Korea invaded South Korea. From 1950-1953, the Soviet Union and China aided

North Korea and the United Nations aided South Korea in this war. It ended in a stalemate, with the country split in two at the 38th parallel.

9. Kim-Il sung: He was the leader of communist North Korea and ordered the invasion of South Korea in 1950.

10. Ho Chi Minh: He was a Communist leader of North Vietnam and Vietnam from 1935 until his death in 1969.

11. Vietnam War: The United States of America fought against communist Vietnam from 1963-1973. The war ended in a stalemate. In 1975, communist North Vietnam conquered South Vietnam. Communist North Vietnam then murdered more than 1,000,000 South Vietnamese who were against communists, and many more escaped or died trying to escape Communist Vietnam.

12. Ronald Reagan: United States President from 1981-1989, Reagan strongly opposed Communism and tried to defeat the Soviet Union.

13. Berlin Wall: The Communists built this wall to keep Communist citizens from escaping to freedom. Germans eventually took down the wall in 1991. Soviet and Eastern European Communists lost power in 1991.

Part IV

American History

51. The Discovery of America

Christopher Columbus (1451-1506) discovered America. He was an explorer, cartographer (map maker), and adventurer from the Republic of Genoa (today part of northern Italy). In **1492**, he led an expedition from Spain and discovered the islands of the West Indies. He died believing he had found a westerly route to Asia, but in reality, he had opened up the continents of North America and South America for European discovery and colonization. Columbus Day is a federal holiday and is celebrated on October 12, 1492, the day he landed in America.

Before Columbus, others had discovered America and others were actually living in America. However, none of the pre-Columbian discoveries had any impact on the rest of the world. In the Medieval Ages, The Vikings travelled to North America centuries before Columbus. **Eric the Red** (c. 950-1003), a Norsemen, established a Viking colony in Greenland. However, his colony disappeared. Native Americans had lived in America for thousands of years before Columbus came, but, nobody else in the world knew of the existence of North and South America because of the Indians.

In 1492, **King Ferdinand II and Queen Isabella I of Spain**, fresh from their victory over the Muslims in the Reconquista, agreed to allow the explorer Christopher Columbus to use Spanish ships and men to go on his quest. Columbus set out in three ships: the *Niña*, **the** *Pinta*, **and the** *Santa Maria*. His goals were to find a new trade route to Asia, to find gold and bring it back to Spain, to map and explore the land he reached, to claim new land for Spain, and to spread Catholic Christianity throughout the world. Columbus believed that by sailing west from Spain, he would eventually arrive in India. After approximately 30 days, Columbus found land. However, as we know, it was not Asia; it was an island in the Bahamas. Columbus believed he had found India and called the natives "Indians."

Columbus made four separate journeys to the **Bahamas**. Columbus' men were so intent on finding gold that they mistreated many Indians. Historical accounts document torture and murder by some of Columbus' men. Columbus was either unable or unwilling to stop them. The Spanish king and queen arrested Columbus, had him brought him back to Spain in chains, tried him for incompetence and for the cruel treatment some of his men perpetrated against the Indians, and jailed him.

Columbus' legacy in the New World is mixed. He discovered America and opened up new lands for the rest of the world. Before Columbus, Indians in the Americas worshipped multiple gods, many practiced torture and **polygamy**, and some practiced **cannibalism** as a way of life. Europeans who came and settled the Americas brought monotheism and ended polygamy. The European immigrants established the United States of America and all other countries of North and South America. Unfortunately, the group of Indians Columbus first encountered, the **Tainos**, were extinct 50 years later. Most Indians who came into contact with the Spanish and other Europeans died from new diseases, such as **smallpox**.

Facts to Know for the Discovery of America

1. Christopher Columbus: Christopher Columbus (1451-1506) was an Italian explorer who discovered America for Spain in 1492.

2. 1492: In 1492, Columbus discovered America.

3. Eric the Red: Around 1000, Eric the Red led a group of Norsemen from Iceland and founded a colony on Greenland, in North America.

4. King Ferdinand II and Queen Isabella I: King Ferdinand II and Queen Isabella I of Spain commissioned Columbus to sail the Atlantic Ocean and find a westerly route to Asia.

5. The *Niña*, the *Pinta*, and the *Santa Maria:* The *Niña*, the *Pinta*, and the *Santa Maria* were the three ships Columbus sailed on his first journey to America.

6. The Bahamas: The Bahamas are a series of islands that Columbus first discovered. They are located south of Florida.

7. Polygamy: Polygamy is the practice of having multiple wives at the same time.

8. Cannibalism: Cannibalism is the practice of humans eating humans.

9. Tainos: The Tainos were the Indians Columbus and his men encountered in their journeys to America. The Tainos were extinct 50 years after coming into contact with Columbus.

10. Smallpox: Smallpox is a disease that can be deadly. The Indians first encounter with smallpox was when they came into contact with the Spaniards. Historians think 90% of the Indians died of smallpox.

52. Native Americans

Native Americans, or Indians, lived throughout North and South America when European explorers and settlers came into contact with them. Indians who lived in what became the United States of America lacked a written language, used Stone Age tools because they lacked knowledge to form metal into productive uses, were similar to pre-Hebraic cultures in that they were **polytheistic** (believed in many gods), and had minimal protections against disease and wild animals. Most Indians practiced slavery, and a man could have as many wives as he could feed through his hunting. Commonly, a victorious Indian tribe captured all women in a defeated tribe and forced them to become wives. One interesting fact about the people we call Native Americans, or Indians, is that even their ancestors migrated to the Americas. So, like all other people in the United States, Indians can trace their ancestry to other continents.

Geography and climate greatly influenced Indians because of their lack of technology. They lived in either agricultural, **nomadic**, hunting, or fishing tribal societies. There were over 300 tribes, each with its own language and customs, within the area of the present-day United States of America. In this area, anthropologists identify three cultural groups: **Woodland** (East of the Mississippi River), **Plains**, and **Coastal** (West Coast) Indians. Woodland Indians were agricultural, and Plains and Coastal Indians were hunters and gatherers.

Woodland Indians were the first that early settlers of America confronted. Male Indians were farmers, hunters, and fishermen, and they made war and gambled, while the Indian women did all of the gathering of fruits, nuts, and roots, the cooking, the raising of the children, and were in charge of the home. Indians, in constant conflict with other tribes, engaged in unwritten treaties for protection. When the European settlers came, Indians viewed them as another Indian tribe, with some tribes becoming allies of the Europeans, and other tribes attempting to destroy them. Woodland Indians fished from the shores of the Great Lakes to the Atlantic Coast. The largest of these tribes formed the **Iroquois League,** a loose confederation where the tribes agreed to come to each other's defense if one were attacked. Tribes of the Woodlands practiced balance of power politics, allying with other tribes to guarantee their survival.

Other Indians of North America included Plains, Coastal, Southwest, and Arctic. Indians of the Arctic were fishermen and lived in underground houses or igloos on the Pacific or Arctic coasts. Subarctic Indians gathered plants, fished, trapped animals, and hunted mostly caribou. **California Indians,** fisherman, hunters and gatherers, lived in either small huts or wooden homes. Northwest Coastal Indians were fishermen who lived in wooden houses. Southwest tribes such as the **Navajo** were an exception to the rule: even though they were close to the Plains, they were farmers of beans and corn and lived in homes made of adobe. Plains Indians initially hunted buffalo on foot. Starting in 1492, Columbus and the Spanish introduced **horses** to America. Some escaped and were captured by the Plains Indians, who then used these animals to hunt.

Facts to Know for Native Americans

1. Native Americans: Native Americans, or Indians, lived throughout North and South America when European explorers and settlers came into contact with them.

2. Polytheism: Polytheism means the belief in many gods.

3. Nomad: A nomad does not have a permanent home, but follows the animal herds.

4. Woodland Indians: Woodland Indians live east of the Mississippi River, lived in wooden longhouses, and were the first the Europeans came into contact with when Europeans came to America.

5. Plains Indians: Plains Indians lived on the American Plains. They initially hunted buffalo on foot. Starting in 1492, Columbus and the Spanish introduced horses to America. Some escaped and were captured by the Plains Indians, who then used these animals to hunt.

6. Coastal Indians: Coastal Indians were fisherman, hunters and gatherers, and lived in either small huts or wooden homes. Northwest Coastal Indians were fishermen who lived in wooden houses.

7. Iroquois League: The Iroquois League was a loose confederation where the tribes agreed to come to each other's defense if one were attacked. They were Woodland Indians.

53. Spanish Colonies in North America

Because of Christopher Columbus, Spain was the first country to take advantage of the possibilities in the new land. Throughout the 1500s, 1600s, and 1700s, Spain sent explorers, colonizers, and Catholic missionaries to the Americas. They established Spain as the greatest presence in the New World before England would even begin to expand. However, the Spanish colonists lacked the freedom and opportunities of the English colonists, and the Spanish colonies in North America would never become as successful as the English colonies. The Spanish Empire was gigantic, but Spain's importance in what became the United States of America was limited. The **Spanish Empire in North America** encompassed the Southwest, Florida, Texas, and all of Mexico and Central America.

On August 28, 1565, Spanish explorers sighted land while off the coast of present-day Florida. Because the sailors of Spain were Catholic, they founded a city on this land and named it after the saint day of August 28, **Saint Augustine**. They built a fort, and had a meal of thanksgiving to God, the first thanksgiving meal in North America, though not the most famous and most important one.

The Spanish had been incredibly successful in finding gold among the **Aztecs** in Mexico and the **Incas** in South America in the 1500s, and they thought that gold had to be further north as well. To find this gold, **Hernando de Soto** explored the Southeast and discovered the Mississippi River. **Francisco Coronado** went in search of the fabled "Seven Cities" of gold in the Southwest, but instead discovered the Grand Canyon. The failure of the Spanish to find gold led them to focus their efforts on colonizing what would become Mexico and South America.

Many Spanish came to America not for gold, but to spread Christianity among the Indians. Spanish missionaries established missions, learned Indian languages that had never before been written down, and in some cases, were tortured and killed by the Indians. **Bartolome de Las Casas** came to America initially to get rich in the 1500s, but he gave up this desire and became a Catholic priest. For over 50 years, he defended the rights of the Indians, successfully arguing against using Indians as slaves. Also in the 1500s, **Father Luis de Cancer** went to Florida to convert the Indians, though they rejected his message and scalped him. (To **scalp** someone means to chop off a chunk of the back of the skull, killing the person.) In the 1700s, **Father Junipero Serra** established the California missions, a string of 21 settlements that served as churches, hospitals, and centers of agriculture and industry.

Facts to Know for Spanish Colonies in North America

1. Spanish Empire in North America: The Spanish Empire in North America encompassed the Southwest, Florida, Texas, and all of Mexico and Central America.

2. Saint Augustine: On August 28, 1565, Spanish established Saint Augustine, the oldest European settlement on the North American mainland. The Spanish held the first Thanksgiving in America that very year.

3. Aztecs: The Aztecs were an Indian nation in present-day Mexico who controlled a large area of land and other Indian nations. The Spanish conquered the Aztecs in the 1500s, under the leadership of Hernando Cortes.

4. Incas: The Incass were an Indian nation in present-day Peru who controlled a large area of land and other Indian nations. The Spanish conquered the Incas in the 1500s, under the leadership of Francisco Pizarro.

5. Hernando de Soto: To find this gold, Hernando de Soto explored the Southeast and discovered the Mississippi River in the 1500s.

6. Francisco Coronado: Francisco Coronado went in search of the fabled "Seven Cities" of gold in the Southwest, but instead discovered the Grand Canyon in the 1500s.

7. Father Bartolome de Las Casas: Father Bartolome de Las Casas came to America initially to get rich in the 1500s, but he gave up this desire and became a Catholic priest. For

over 50 years, he defended the rights of the Indians, successfully arguing against using Indians as slaves.

8. Father Luis de Cancer: Father Luis de Cancer went to Florida to convert the Indians, though they rejected his message and scalped him.

9. Scalp: To scalp means to kill someone by chopping off the top, back part of a person's head.

10. Father Junipero Serra: In the 1700s, Father Junipero Serra established the California missions, a string of 21 settlements that served as churches, hospitals, and centers of agriculture and industry.

54. French Colonies in North America

Even though Christopher Columbus failed to find a westerly route to Asia, Europeans still believed that there was an all-water route to Asia and searched for a pathway through North America. This path that really did not exist was called the **Northwest Passage**. French explorer **Jacques Cartier** tried to find the Northwest Passage, and in the process discovered a large gulf and river he named the St. Lawrence Gulf and the St. Lawrence River. He also found two Indian villages—one later became Quebec and the other he named Montreal, which means Royal Mountain. Though Cartier thought his journeys had been a failure, France laid claim to the land he discovered and established the French Empire in North America. The French Empire would also lay claim to a large area in the center of what would become the United States of America.

In 1608, **Samuel de Champlain** founded the city of Quebec, located on the banks of the St. Lawrence River in an area perfect for a fort, atop a steep cliff. Champlain wanted to spread Catholicism among the Indians and establish a fur trading settlement that would bring him and France riches. Champlain succeeded in making friends with the **Algonquin and Huron Indians**, but this brought hatred towards New France from the Iroquois Indians who lived in New York and hated the Algonquin Indians. The Iroquois became friends with the English, and thus the French-English rivalry in North America began right at the founding of the new colonies. Because Champlain founded the first successful French settlement in North America, he is called the Father of New France.

Along with setting up fur trading outposts throughout what would become Canada, the French sent missionaries to the Indians to teach them about Jesus Christ. **Father Isaac Jogues** left Quebec and travelled over 900 miles by canoe and on foot to the Mohawk Indians. On the journey, the **Mohawks**, one of the tribes of the Iroquois, captured Jogues and his friend. The Mohawks killed his friend and tortured Jogues before he could escape. The Mohawks bit off Jogues' fingers, forced sticks up his wounds up to his elbow, and beat him all over his body. After his torture, he was made a slave. He then escaped and went back to France. Safely in France, Jogues chose to go back to Canada to try to convert the Indians, was captured by the Mohawks again, and this time they murdered him.

The French sent missionaries and explorers down the **Mississippi River,** established forts along this largest river system in North America, and laid claim to a giant territory in North America. **Father Jacques Marquette and Louis Joliet** explored and mapped much of the Mississippi River in the 1600s. In the late 1600s, **Robert de la Salle** wanted to build a huge French fur trading empire in North America. He took an exploring party and mapped the Mississippi River Valley, claiming it all for France. He named it **Louisiana,** in honor of the French King Louis XIV, in 1682.

Facts to Know for French Colonies in North America

1. Northwest Passage: Europeans believed that there was an all-water route to Asia and searched for a pathway through North America. This path that really did not exist was called the Northwest Passage.

2. Jacques Cartier: Jacques Cartier tried to find the Northwest Passage, and in the process discovered a large gulf and river he named the St. Lawrence Gulf and the St. Lawrence River.

3. Samuel de Champlain: In 1608, Samuel de Champlain founded the city of Quebec. He is called the Father of New France.

4. Algonquin and Huron Indians: Algonquin and Huron Indians became friends with the French. The Algonquin and Huron were enemies of the Iroquois. The Iroquois were friends with the English. This made the Algonquin and Huron enemies of the English, and the Iroquois enemies of the French.

5. Father Isaac Jogues: Father Isaac Jogues left Quebec and travelled over 900 miles by canoe and on foot to the Mohawk Indians to spread Christianity. The Mohawk Indians tortured and murdered Jogues.

6. Mohawks: The Mohawks were one of the tribes of the Iroquois.

7. Mississippi River: The Mississippi River system is the largest in North America.

8. Father Jacques Marquette and Louis Joliet: Father Jacques Marquette and Louis Joliet explored and mapped much of the Mississippi River in the 1600s.

9. Robert de la Salle: In the late 1600s, Robert de la Salle wanted to build a huge French fur trading empire in North America. He took an exploring party and mapped the Mississippi River Valley, claiming it all for France.

10. Louisiana: Robert de la Salle explores and names an area Louisiana, in honor of the French King Louis XIV, in 1682.

55. The Founding of Jamestown, Part I

The first successful English colony in North America was the 1607 settlement of **Jamestown**, in the colony of Virginia. Seeing the riches Spain taken from North and South America, the English wanted to join in. But instead of being led by the English government, the English colonies received their start from private citizens, through a type of business called a joint-stock company. Individual investors founded the **London Company** in 1607 and received approval from **King James I** to found a settlement in Virginia. The company chose a governor and colonists were employees. Most were gold-seeking gentlemen adventurers who thought physical labor beneath them.

Instead of a paradise, the land of America was a nightmare for the first settlers of Jamestown. Out of 120 colonists, more than two-thirds died the first winter. They died of malnutrition, malaria, other diseases, and brackish water, and were attacked by Indians who viewed the English as another tribe to oppose. In 1608, **Captain John** Smith assumed control of Jamestown and imposed military discipline. He made this rule, "He who will not work will not eat." Smith organized raids on Indians, which brought the settlers food, but also more hatred toward them. But in the second winter, in 1608, less than 15% of the settlers died. After that winter, Smith was injured and sent back to England.

In the winter of 1609, the settlers experienced the harshest conditions imaginable. The London Company, now called **The Virginia Company**, had sent ships from England bringing people and supplies, increasing the population to nearly 500. There was not enough food for the people, and the Indians, intent on destroying the new settlement, attacked anyone who stepped outside. Settlers ate everything possible that winter, known as the **Starving Time**. Their meals were rats, mice, snakes, toadstools, horses, and even dead humans. When a supply ship arrived in the spring of 1610, only 60 of the 490 settlers were still alive.

For the next five years, **Sir Thomas Dale**, a cruel and exacting man, led Jamestown. He drove away some of the Indians and built fortifications. He punished settlers for not working hard enough by whippings and putting them to work in irons (chains) for years. Those who rebelled were executed by being tortured, starved to death, or burned to death.

Pocahontas is perhaps the most well-known of the Indians during the beginnings of Jamestown. She was one of **Chief Powhatan**'s hundred (or hundreds) of children, but reportedly his favorite. As a child, Pocahontas had played with the boys within Jamestown. When she was a young woman of 16, English Captain Samuel Argall paid Indian Chief Japasaw a copper kettle to capture her. The Jamestown settlers held Pocahontas captive so Chief Powhatan would stop attacking the settlers. In Jamestown, Pocahontas chose to become a Christian and was baptized. **John Rolfe** married her, they had a son, and Pocahontas went to England, where she was treated as a princess. On her return voyage to America, Pocahontas died of tuberculosis.

Facts to Know for The Founding of Jamestown, Part I

1. Jamestown: In 1607, the English founded the first successful English settlement in America. The English named it Jamestown, in the colony of Virginia.

2. The London Company: The London Company financed the settlement of Virginia.

3. King James I: King James I (1566-1625) gave the London Company approval to settle Virginia.

4. Captain John Smith: In 1608, Captain John Smith assumed control of Jamestown and imposed military discipline. Many argue he saved the young colony.

5. The Virginia Company: In 1609, the London Company became the Virginia Company.

6. The Starving Time: From 1609 to the spring of 1610, 430 of 490 English settlers died in Jamestown.

7. Sir Thomas Dale: From 1610 to 1615, Sir Thomas Dale ruled Jamestown with an iron fist. Attempting to discipline the settlers, Dale beats, tortures, and kills those who go against him.

8. Pocahantas: Pocahantas was the Indian daughter of Chief Powhatan. She was captured by the English at Jamestown. She became a Christian and married John Rolfe. She visited London, was treated as a princess, and caught tuberculosis and died.

9. Chief Powhatan: Chief Powhatan was the strongest Indian leader when Jamestown was founded in 1607. He traded and fought with the English. His daughter was Pocahantas.

10. John Rolfe: John Rolfe was the Englishman who married Pocahantas.

56. The Founding of Jamestown, Part II

The first settlers of Jamestown believed they would find gold treasures that matched or surpassed those found by the Spanish among the **Aztecs and Incas**, but there was little or no gold to be found. However, the Indians introduced them to a plant that came to be the moneymaker of Virginia and other southern colonies—tobacco. **Tobacco** is an addictive stimulant that can be sniffed, chewed, or smoked. It soon became very popular in Europe, and was a very popular drug in America until the 1980s.

In November of 1618, everything changed for the people of Jamestown and the Virginia Colony when the Virginia Company granted a "Great Charter" to the people living in Virginia. Before the Great Charter, Jamestown was organized as a **commune**. A common warehouse fed and clothed everyone, which was a disincentive to work because the laziest man received the same amount as the most industrious. There was never enough food, and life was harsh under the military laws, making Virginia a very unpopular place to go.

Under the new **Great Charter of Virginia**, the colonists were allowed a voice in their government. Virginia was granted a governor, a council, and a general assembly. The property holders of Virginia elected the general assembly, known as the **House of Burgesses**. It was the first group of elected lawmakers in North American history. In 1623, the Virginia Company went bankrupt, and after that the King of England chose the governor and the council. Virginia had the freest people in the world, outside of England. Everywhere else, a ruler dictated to the people what they had to do. In Jamestown, free government in America was born.

The Great Charter of Virginia also contained major changes involving **private property** and how an individual could support himself. It divided the land of Virginia into farms, and each man received the right to own land and work for himself. Immediately, industrious people in Virginia set out to work, and their colony saw huge improvements in its economy. Virginia became an attraction for many English people. In England, land was scarce and extremely expensive, and in Virginia, every owner of land had the right to vote. These two aspects made Virginia, and America, exceptions to the worldwide rule. Nowhere else could a person of humble means own land, prosper, and vote.

In **1619**, one year after the Great Charter, two major social changes came to Virginia. Women arrived, and slave traders brought African slaves. Unlike the French, the English colonists normally would not marry Indian women. The arrival of English females meant the colony would grow on its own. To marry, a man had to gain consent from a woman, and then he had to pay her passage from England with **150 pounds of tobacco.** With the arrival of slaves began the divisive slave issue in America that ended with the Civil War over two hundred years later.

Facts to Know for The Founding of Jamestown, Part II

1. Aztecs and Incas: The Aztecs and Incas were Native Americans from present-day Mexico and Peru. In the 1500s, the Spanish conquered the Aztecs and Incas and took much gold.

2. Tobacco: Tobacco is an addictive stimulant that can be sniffed, chewed, or smoked. American Indians introduced it to the English in Virginia. It soon became very popular in Europe, and was a very popular drug in America until the 1980s.

3. Commune: In a commune, nobody owns any property individually. Everything is shared, including work, food, and any product of the community.

4. The Great Charter of Virginia: The Great Charter of Virginia of 1618 allowed the Jamestown settlers to own private property and to have the power to vote and elect lawmakers for Virginia.

5. The House of Burgesses: The House of Burgesses was the first elected body of lawmakers in North America, in Jamestown, Virginia.

6. Private Property: Private property is property that is owned by an individual. In Europe in the 1700s, only the nobility could own property. In Jamestown, every citizen could own private property.

7. 1619: In 1619, slaves were brought to and women came to Jamestown, Virginia.

8. 150 pounds of tobacco: In Jamestown, 150 pounds of tobacco was the price a man had to pay a ship captain to buy his bride.

57. Founding of Plymouth Plantation

In the early 1600s, a group of people called **Pilgrims** left England to find a new home where they could practice their religion freely. In England, the government persecuted everyone who was not a member of the Church of England (Anglican). The Pilgrims were Protestants but not **Anglicans**. They went to **Holland**, where there was religious freedom. In Holland, the Pilgrims could practice their religion freely, but they were not happy. Their children were learning to speak Dutch, practice Dutch customs, and were losing their English identity. Also, in England, the Pilgrims had been farmers, but in Holland, they lived in cities. Because of these reasons, the Pilgrims decided to leave Holland.

After returning to England for a short time, the Pilgrims left for America in **1620**. The King of England had allowed them to settle in Virginia. While at sea, a storm hit, and they sailed off course, over 600 miles north of Jamestown. After traveling 65 days, they landed their ship, **the** *Mayflower*, in the New World. Before stepping ashore, they wrote **the Mayflower Compact**, a short paper declaring every person's intention to glorify God, follow the laws, and to honor the King of England. They wanted to make it clear to the king they were not intentionally founding a settlement far from Virginia. The Mayflower Compact was the first self-written constitution in North America.

102 English citizens set foot in America and founded **Plymouth**, in present-day Massachusetts. The Pilgrims stayed on their ship until they could build homes out of the wood from the forest.   At Plymouth Plantation, the first

year was incredibly harsh for the Pilgrims. They settled on abandoned Indian fields. Of the 102 settlers, 45 died within a few months. Of the 18 women, only 4 survived that first year. The Pilgrims were unaccustomed to the harsh winters of the Northeast, and did not know which crops grew best. Afraid of the Indians, who had attacked a Pilgrim exploring party, the Pilgrims leveled and planted corn over the graves when they buried their dead. They did this so the Indians would not know how weak the Pilgrims were.

One day in spring, an Indian man named **Samoset** walked up to the Pilgrims, and to their surprise, said, "Welcome, Englishmen." Samoset had learned English from English fishermen, who travelled to the American coast for the abundant fishing. He introduced the Pilgrims to **Squanto**, who had lived among English speakers for a time as a slave. When Squanto regained his freedom, he went back to his people in America. Squanto taught the Pilgrims what crops to grow and how to use fish as a fertilizer. He also acted as a peaceful contact between the Pilgrims and the most powerful Indian of the area, **Chief Massasoit**.

In Plymouth Plantation, just as in Jamestown, the settlers first tried to share everything, including land, work, clothing, food and drink. There were always shortages, and there were those who would not work and so benefitted from the work of others. In 1624, Plymouth Plantation introduced **private property**. Each family received its own land, and from that time on, Plymouth Plantation was a success. The industrious worked hard, saved, and grew in wealth and in self-sufficiency.

Facts to Know for the Founding of Plymouth Plantation

1. Pilgrims: Pilgrims are religious people on a journey. In American history, the Pilgrims were those who founded Plymouth.

2. Anglicans: The only legal church in 1620England was The Church of England. Members of this church were called Anglicans.

3. Holland: The Pilgrims left England to live in Holland. They were allowed to live there, but their children were adopting Dutch customs, and they wanted their children to remain English.

4. 1620: In 1620, the Pilgrims left England to go to America.

5. The Mayflower: The Mayflower was the name of the ship the Pilgrims took to America in 1620.

6. The Mayflower Compact: Pilgrims wrote the Mayflower Compact in 1620. It is the first self-written governing document in North America.

7. Plymouth: Plymouth, also known as Plymouth Plantation, was founded by the Pilgrims in 1620. It is located in present-day Massachusetts.

8. Samoset and Squanto: Samoset and Squanto were American Indians who helped the Pilgrims by showing them how to use fish as fertilizer when planting corn.

9. Chief Massasoit: Chief Massasoit was the most powerful Indian near where the Pilgrims lived.

10. Private Property: Once Pilgrims allowed individuals to own private property, Plymouth Plantation became successful.

58. The First Thanksgiving

In the **fall of 1621**, the Pilgrims, a very religious people, decided to set aside a time to honor God and give him thanks for all of their blessings. It is amazing to think of the faith, courage, and humility of these people. In the previous year, half of them had died in a cold and cruel climate. They were far from their friends and comforts. And still, they wanted to set aside several days to give God thanks for their blessings. They invited their neighbors, the Indians, to show them thanks for their help, and to include them in their feast.

The first Thanksgiving in America lasted for three days, involved all of the Pilgrims (approximately 50), and 90 Indian men. In the Indian culture of the Northeast, it was common for Indians to steal the wives of enemies, and the Indians thought the Pilgrims would do the same to them, so no Indian women came. During these three days, the Indians played competitive games, and the English and Indian men shared the best foods together.

Two years later, in 1623, the governor of Massachusetts, **William Bradford**, wrote America's first **Thanksgiving Proclamation**. He set aside a specific day and time for the citizens to honor God for his blessings. Beginning with President George Washington, U.S. presidents have issued a Thanksgiving Proclamation as well. In 1863, in the middle of the American Civil War, during which over 600,000 Americans were killed, President Abraham Lincoln declared that the last Thursday in November be set aside as "a day of Thanksgiving and Praise to our beneficent Father who dwelleth in the Heavens." Lincoln's proclamation made **Thanksgiving Day** a federal holiday.

Facts to Know for the First Thanksgiving

1. The fall of 1621: In the fall of 1621, Pilgrims celebrated the first Thanksgiving.

2. William Bradford: In 1623, the governor of Massachusetts, William Bradford, wrote America's first Thanksgiving Proclamation.

3. Thanksgiving Proclamation: Massachusetts governor William Bradford, in 1623, issued the first Thanksgiving Proclamation. President Washington was the first U.S. President to issue a Thanksgiving Proclamation. Every President since has issued a Thanksgiving Proclamation.

4. Thanksgiving Day: In 1863, in the middle of the United States' largest war in terms of American deaths, President Lincoln declared Thanksgiving Day as a federal holiday. Lincoln declared that the last Thursday in November be set aside as "a day of Thanksgiving and Praise to our beneficent Father who dwelleth in the Heavens."

59. The Mayflower Compact and the First Thanksgiving: Primary Sources

The Mayflower Compact, 1620

In the name of God, Amen. We whose names are under-written, the loyal subjects of our dread **sovereign** Lord, King James, by the grace of God, of Great Britain, France, and Ireland King, Defender of the Faith, etc.

Having undertaken, for the glory of God, and advancement of the Christian faith, and honor of our King and Country, a voyage to plant the first colony in the northern parts of Virginia, do by these presents **solemnly** and mutually, in the presence of God, and one of another, covenant and combine our selves together into a **civil body politic**, for our better ordering and preservation and furtherance of the ends aforesaid; and by virtue hereof to enact, constitute, and frame such just and equal laws, ordinances, acts, constitutions and offices, from time to time, as shall be thought most meet and convenient for the general good of the Colony, unto which we promise all due submission and obedience. In witness whereof we have hereunder subscribed our names at Cape Cod, the eleventh of November [New Style, November 21], in the year of the reign of our sovereign lord, King James, of England, France, and Ireland, the eighteenth, and of Scotland the fifty-fourth. Anno Dom. 1620.

America's First Thanksgiving Proclamation by Governor Bradford
1623

Inasmuch as the great Father has given us this year an abundant harvest of Indian corn, wheat, peas, beans, squashes, and garden vegetables, and has made the forests to abound with game and the sea with fish and clams, and inasmuch as he has protected us from the ravages of the savages, has spared us from **pestilence** and disease, has granted us freedom to worship God according to the dictates of our own conscience.

Now I, your **magistrate**, do proclaim that all ye Pilgrims, with your wives and ye little ones, do gather at ye meeting house, on ye hill, between the hours of 9 and 12 in the day time, on Thursday, November 29th, of the year of our Lord one thousand six hundred and twenty-three and the third year since ye Pilgrims landed on ye **Pilgrim Rock**, there to listen to ye pastor and render thanksgiving to ye Almighty God for all His blessings.

Facts to Know for
The Mayflower Compact and the First
Thanksgiving: Primary Sources

1. Sovereign: Sovereign means ruler.

2. Solemnly: Solemnly means when someone does something in a serious manner.

3. Civil Body Politic: The civil body politic means a community that is organized politically.

4. Pestilence: Pestilence means a fatal epidemic disease.

5. Magistrate: Magistrate means a person who is an official who governs.

6. Pilgrim Rock: It is believed that the ship the Mayflower landed either right next to "Pilgrim Rock" or that it slightly bumped "Pilgrim Rock."

60. The Southern Colonies

English colonization in North America began in the South, and at the time of the American Revolution, the Southern colonies had a larger population and economy than the rest of the county. American Founding Fathers **George Washington, Thomas Jefferson, James Madison, and Patrick Henry** all came from Virginia, perhaps the most important colony, alongside Massachusetts.

The Southern colonies were **Georgia, South Carolina, North Carolina, Virginia, and Maryland**. The first settlers of Virginia never did find gold, but what they did find became almost as valuable. Indians introduced the Jamestown colonists to **tobacco**. The English quickly fell in love with the plant that they could smoke or sniff, and tobacco became the currency for most of the settlers in Virginia. If a settler wanted to buy something, he would pay in pounds of tobacco! Without tobacco, the settlement of Virginia and perhaps the success of the English colonies might not have happened.

Climate in the Southern colonies was warm and humid in the summer and mild in the winter, ideal for farming. Broad rivers made it easy to bring crops to market. There are few high mountains and the **Appalachian Mountains** reach no higher than a few thousand feet. The main crops of the South were tobacco, rice, and indigo. In the backcountry beyond the farms, Southerners hunted wild animals.

The Southern colonies started for various reasons. The **London Company** founded Virginia to make a profit for its investors. **Lord Baltimore** established Maryland as a place for Catholics and people of all faiths to worship freely. **King Charles II** founded North and South Carolina to keep the French and Spanish away. Georgia was founded by **James Oglethorpe**, who convinced King George II to allow debtors in English prisons to settle in Georgia, work, and pay off their debt. So when historians write that Georgia was founded by prisoners, they are telling the truth!

Nearly every Southerner worked on a farm. The great majority of white Southern families owned individual small farms. About 5% of Southerners were rich plantation owners. A plantation was a huge farm, where a hundred or more slaves would labor. About **35%-45%** of the Southern colonies' population was slave.

For recreation, Southern whites spent their time horse racing, hunting, dancing, card playing or playing the violin or flute. Children played many games during their free time. In the game "rolling the hoop," each child would roll a wooden hoop and race to a finish line, trying to reach it first. Another game, "pins," was very much like our game of bowling. Children played marbles, hopscotch, leapfrog, and tag.

Facts to Know for The Southern Colonies

1. George Washington, Thomas Jefferson, James Madison, and Patrick Henry: These American Founding Fathers were all from Virginia.

2. The Southern Colonies: The Southern colonies were Georgia, South Carolina, North Carolina, Virginia, and Maryland.

3. Tobacco: Tobacco is an addictive drug the Indians introduced to the settlers of Jamestown. Tobacco was used for currency in Virginia and was a key reason for the success of Virginia.

4. Appalachian Mountains: The Appalachian Mountains stretch north to south from New York to Mississippi.

5. The London Company: The London Company founded the colony of Virginia. It became the Virginia Company.

6. Lord Baltimore: Lord Baltimore established Maryland as a place for Catholics and people of all faiths to worship freely.

7. King Charles II: King Charles II founded North and South Carolina to keep the French and Spanish away.

8. James Oglethorpe: Georgia was founded by James Oglethorpe, who convinced King George II to allow debtors in English prisons to settle in Georgia, work, and pay off their debt.

9. 35%-45%: About 35%-45% of the Southern colonies' population was slave.

10. Southern Crops: The main crops of the South were tobacco, rice, and indigo.

61. French and Indian War (1754-1763)

Throughout the colonial period, England fought France in four major wars in North America. The French had a successful fur trade that the English wanted. The English were Protestant and the French were Roman Catholic. England had a limited monarchy and France had an absolute monarchy. English settlers had many more political rights than French settlers. However, perhaps the greatest difference between the English settlers and the French settlers was their number: there were 16 English for every one Frenchmen in **North America in 1750** (c. 1.6 million English colonists and at most c. 100,000 French).

To send the French a message that the English wanted them out of the Ohio Valley, **Governor Robert Dinwiddie** of Virginia sent a young and capable 21-year-old major in the Virginia militia, **George Washington**. Washington and his men surprised a smaller number of French soldiers. The French attempted to surrender, but Washington's Indian allies would not stop, leaving no Frenchmen alive. Washington then retreated, building **Fort Necessity**. A larger French force attacked with superior power, forcing Washington to surrender, but he wrote later, he "heard the bullets whistle and …there is something charming in the sound."

Throughout the war, George Washington impressed both the English and the colonists, and became recognized as a leader. In one battle, George Washington attempted to warn the British **General Braddock** of the danger of marching with red coats on a narrow path through the forest, and he tried to tell the British how the Indians fought in America. General Braddock dismissed the advice, and at the **Battle**

of Monongahela, Braddock was killed, along with every other officer except Washington. Washington had multiple horses shot from under him, had bullets pierce his vest, yet he still ably led the British in an organized retreat.

Great Britain defeated France in the French and Indian War, and in the **Treaty of Paris in 1763**, received all of the French territory in North America. This meant that Great Britain now controlled all of Canada and the land east of the Mississippi River, and north of Florida and Louisiana. Colonists went home, hoping to return to life without war. As the English moved into the French forts west of the Appalachian Mountains, Indians rose up to fight the newcomers. "**Pontiac's War**" lasted from 1763 to 1764, with the British and colonists defeating the Indians.

The French and Indian War was a costly one on both sides. English and French colonists suffered at the hands of each other's armies and the Indians. Both sides committed atrocities. Various Indian tribes allied themselves with each country, and raided both French and English villages, killing soldiers and civilians alike. English officers would not listen to advice from colonial soldiers regarding ways to fight in the forest, and the colonists lost more men than necessary. The English borrowed large amounts of money, and by the end of the war, had a huge debt. To pay the **war debt**, the English Parliament and **King George III** planned to levy a series of taxes on the colonists. They incorrectly believed Americans would pay the taxes out of gratitude for the British defeat of France.

Facts to Know for the French and Indian War (1754-1763)

1. European population of North America in 1750: In North America in 1750, there were c. 1.6 million English colonists and at most c. 100,000 French.

2. Governor Robert Dinwiddie: Governor Robert Dinwiddie (1692-1770) was the governor of colonial Virginia during the French and Indian War.

3. George Washington: George Washington (1732-1799) was an able colonial officer during the French and Indian War.

4. Fort Necessity: In the Ohio River Valley, during the French and Indian War, Washington and his soldiers built Fort Necessity, but surrendered it to the French.

5. General Braddock: General Braddock (1695-1755) was one of the most respected British generals at the beginning of the French and Indian War. He was killed at the Battle of Monongahela.

6. Battle of Monongahela: At the Battle of Monongahela (1755), General Braddock was killed, along with every other officer except Washington. Washington had multiple horses shot from under him, had bullets pierce his vest, yet he still ably led the British in an organized retreat.

7. Treaty of Paris in 1763: In the Treaty of Paris in 1763, Great Britain took control of all of North America.

8. Pontiac's War: As the English moved into the French forts west of the Appalachian Mountains, Indians rose up to fight the newcomers. "Pontiac's War" lasted from 1763 to 1764, with the British and colonists defeating the Indians.

9. War Debt: As a result of the French and Indian War, Great Britain had great debt.

10. King George III: King George III (ruled 1760-1819) was the ruler of Great Britain during the French and Indian War and during the American Revolution.

62. Land Proclamation of 1763

British land regulation and new taxes angered the Americans so much that it is not a far stretch to argue that they caused the American Revolution. Great Britain passed the **Land Proclamation of 1763**, along with a series of taxes. The Americans saw both of these as hostile, which ultimately led the colonists to unite and fight for their freedom.

For two main reasons, the British passed the Proclamation of 1763 which forbade colonists from traveling west of the **Appalachian Mountains**. Although the English won this land in the French and Indian War, they could not secure the safety of the colonists from the Indians, and in fact, the British had promised this land to the Indians. Great Britain also wanted to keep the colonists within its control, and it was easier to do this east of the mountain range. The colonists resented the Proclamation, and openly broke it.

One of these colonists was **Daniel Boone** (1734-1820), a brave explorer and adventurer who achieved legendary status as an American **backwoodsman**. Growing up on the colonial frontier, Boone learned how to be a hunter from the age of 12. As a young man, Boone went on months-long hunting expeditions, shooting bear and deer. He fought in the French and Indian War and was an officer during the Revolutionary War. After buying land from the Cherokee Indians in 1775, the **Transylvania Company** hired Boone to blaze a trail through the Appalachian Mountains, called the **Wilderness Road**. By 1800, over 200,000 people had used this road to travel into present-day Kentucky. Boone also established **Boonesborough**, Kentucky, the first colonial settlement west of the mountains. After the Revolutionary War, he led settlers inland and established new towns. Travelling into the Indian land of present-day Kentucky was dangerous. Indians were upset at outsiders encroaching upon their land, and felt that Indian land had to be defended against the white settlers. While leading a group of about 50 British colonists, Daniel Boone's son James and others were captured by the Indians, then tortured and killed. During his lifetime, Boone was captured by Indians multiple times.

Facts to Know for the
Land Proclamation of 1763

1. Land Proclamation of 1763: Land Proclamation of 1763 was a British law that forbade colonists from crossing over the Appalachian Mountains.

2. Appalachian Mountains: The Appalachian Mountains are the principle mountain range that runs north and south in the east of the United States of America.

3. Daniel Boone (1734-1820): Boone was a brave explorer and adventurer who achieved legendary status as an American backwoodsman.

4. Backwoodsman: A backwoodsman was a man who lived on the frontier. He most likely knew how to use gun, conducted much manual labor, and was not formally educated.

5. The Transylvania Company: In 1775, the Transylvania Company hired Boone to blaze a trail through the Appalachian Mountains, called the Wilderness Road.

6. The Wilderness Road: The Wilderness Road was the trail that Daniel Boone opened up so settlers could move west, over the Appalachian Mountains.

7. Boonesborough was the town Boone established. It was the first permanent settlement west of the Appalachian Mountains.

63. British Taxes and the Americans

While westerners were upset with the British regulations regarding land, colonists along the Atlantic coast were angry about the **Navigation Acts**, a series of laws that limited Americans' sailing and trading rights. Americans were not allowed to trade directly with any country but Great Britain. Americans could not manufacture their own goods and could buy goods only from England. The Navigation Acts caused the politicians in the colonial assemblies, such as James Otis, Samuel Adams, and Patrick Henry, to forcefully assert the colonists' duty to start a revolution.

The **Sugar Act of 1764** and the **Stamp Act of 1765** also caused problems in the colonies. The Sugar Act was the first time the British taxed the colonies purely to raise money. The Stamp Act required all colonists to pay for a British stamp on every legal document. All marriage certificates, legal documents, newspapers, and even playing cards had to have a British stamp that cost a fee. The Stamp Act angered the colonists so much that colonists tried to break the law at every opportunity. An underground economy flourished, with playing cards and other paper items sold without the stamp.

Some Americans viewed the Sugar Act and the Stamp Act as a threat to their rights as Englishmen. **Patrick Henry**, a representative in the **Virginia House of Burgesses**, argued that the right to tax Virginians belonged solely to Virginia's representatives. He condemned the king and Parliament for their actions. Henry stated, "Caesar had his Brutus, Charles the First his Cromwell, and George the Third—" At this point, some representatives in the House of Burgesses were shocked and shouted, "**Treason**! Treason!" The punishment for treason was execution. Patrick Henry answered, "If this be treason, make the most of it." Eventually, Parliament repealed the Stamp Act.

After Great Britain repealed the Stamp Act, the king and Parliament moved quickly and passed other taxes on the Americans, and ordered British troops to occupy certain American cities. The **Quartering Act of 1765** compelled colonists to house British soldiers and to pay for their food and housing. The **Townshend Acts of 1767** were a series of laws that included taxes on many imported items such as tea, paper, lead, and glass. These items were not made in America and the colonists could only buy them from Great Britain.

In manifold response to these taxes, colonists voiced their opinions in their assemblies, wrote editorials in their newspapers, smuggled in items from other countries, **boycotted** British goods, and began to speak openly about the possibility of going to war against Great Britain. They also formed **Committees of Correspondence**, groups of leaders in each colony who wrote each other so that Americans knew what was happening in every part of the country. The equivalent today would be a type of social media where people could share common ideas.

Facts to Know for British Taxes and the Americans

1. The Navigation Acts: The Navigation Acts were a series of laws that severely limited Americans' sailing and trading rights.

2. The Sugar Act of 1764: The Sugar Act of 1764 placed a tax on sugar. It was the first time the British taxed a product in America only to raise income.

3. The Stamp Act of 1765: The Stamp Act of 1765 required all colonists to pay for a British stamp on every legal document.

4. Patrick Henry: Patrick Henry was a representative in the Virginia House of Burgesses who forcefully argued for revolution against the British.

5. Virginia House of Burgesses: The Virginia House of Burgesses was the oldest representative law-making body in America.

6. The Quartering Act of 1765: The Quartering Act of 1765 compelled colonists to house British soldiers and to pay for their food and housing.

7. Townshend Acts of 1767: The Townshend Acts of 1767 were a series of laws that included taxes on many imported items such as tea, paper, lead, and glass. These items were not made in America and the colonists could only buy them from Great Britain.

8. Boycott: To boycott means to not buy something in order to protest and punish the manufacturer of the product.

9. Committees of Correspondence: Committees of Correspondence were groups of leaders in each colony who wrote each other so that Americans knew what was happening in every part of the country.

10. Treason: Treason is an act of grave disloyalty against one's own country.

64. The Boston Massacre and the Boston Tea Party

By 1770, King George III placed British soldiers in Boston, both as a show of force and as a way to protect British tax collectors. Colonial leaders viewed these soldiers as an **occupying force**, and sought for ways to foment anger among all the colonists. The soldiers and the colonists came to violence. British soldiers were standing on patrol in the city when an American mob started throwing snowballs, then rocks, and yelling and screaming at the soldiers. To protect themselves, the British shot at the colonists, killing five and wounding six. Sam Adams labeled this incident **"The Boston Massacre,"** **Paul Revere** engraved a picture of fierce soldiers firing into an unsuspecting crowd, and the picture was reprinted throughout the colonies. Though **John Adams** would represent the soldiers and defend them successfully in court, Americans believed the British to be violent oppressors.

One of the key events preceding the American Revolution, the **Boston Tea Party** (1773) captures the mood of the colonists, the impotence of the British, and the respect some Americans had for private property. Merchant ships brought tea into Boston Harbor. The **Townshend Acts** placed a tax on all imports, including tea. However, the British attempted to make this tax "easier to swallow" by making it so low that the cost of the tea on board the ship was lower than tea sold in Boston stores. Afraid Americans would buy this tea and thus pay the tax, a group of about 60 Bostonians, called the **Sons of Liberty**, dressed up as Indians, boarded the ships, and dumped the tea into the harbor. The incident outraged Benjamin Franklin because it injured the private company who owned the tea. **Robert**

Murray, a New York merchant, offered to pay for the tea, but the British turned him down.

To punish the colonists for the Boston Tea Party, Parliament passed the **Coercive Acts**, known as the "Intolerable Acts" in the colonies. Great Britain took away Massachusetts' self-government, closed the port of Boston, declared that all royal officials accused of crime be tried outside of the colonies, and forced colonists to house and pay for British soldiers with the passing of the **Quartering Act of 1774**. The British hoped that these laws would punish and isolate the wrongdoers in Boston, but instead, they caused many other colonists to go against Great Britain. The Intolerable Acts united the colonies like no other colonial argument could have.

Facts to Know for the Boston Massacre and the Boston Tea Party

1. Occupying Force: The British became an occupying force in Boston, placing soldiers in the town to control the Americans.

2. The Boston Massacre: In the Boston Massacre (1770), acting in self-defense, British soldiers fired on American colonists, killing five. American colonists falsely slandered the British soldiers, calling it a massacre.

3. Paul Revere: Paul Revere (1735-1818) was a silversmith. He designed the sketch and painting that made it appear the British were happy to shoot the Bostonians.

4. John Adams: John Adams (1735-1826) was a lawyer who volunteered to represent the accused British soldiers. He successfully defended them in court.

5. Boston Tea Party (1773): In the Boston Tea Party, colonists protested the Tea Tax by throwing tea into the Boston Harbor.

6. The Townshend Acts: The Townshend Acts were a series of taxes levied on the colonists.

7. The Sons of Liberty: The Sons of Liberty were young men who carried out acts of protest against the British. It was the Sons of Liberty who threw the tea into the Boston Harbor.

8. Robert Murray: Robert Murray, a New York merchant, offered to pay for the tea, but the British turned him down.

Murray and Benjamin Franklin were angry that the colonists destroyed private property.

9. The Coercive Acts: The Coercive Acts were known as the "Intolerable Acts" in the colonies. Great Britain took away Massachusetts' self-government, closed the port of Boston, declared that all royal officials accused of crime be tried outside of the colonies, and forced colonists to house and pay for British soldiers with the passing of the Quartering Act of 1774.

10. The Quartering Act: The Quartering Act forced colonists to house and feed British soldiers.

65. The Ideas of Revolution

As written in *A Patriot's History of the United States*, two main streams of thought permeated the Americans' desire to risk their lives by going to war against Great Britain: **Enlightenment** ideas and Christianity. The theories of three thinkers of the Enlightenment, **Thomas Hobbes**, **John Locke**, and **Baron Charles de Montesquieu**, laid the groundwork for representative government. **Adam Smith** laid the philosophical foundation for the free market, an economic way of life that became America's engine of its first century and a half and transformed one of the world's weakest countries to the world's strongest.

Englishman Thomas Hobbes (1588-1679) wrote in his book *Leviathan* that man's life, without government, was "solitary, poor, nasty, brutish, and short." Government was created to protect life, and a monarch could have absolute power to do this. American colonists liked Hobbes' ideas that government was necessary to protect life. Englishman John Locke (1632-1704) wrote that government's job was to be limited to protecting life, liberty, and property. With a limited role, people would have maximum liberty. French author Montesquieu (1689-1755) wrote that to limit the abuse of power, government should be broken into three branches. Each branch would be responsible for some power, and each would make sure the other branches did not get too much control. Adam Smith (1723-1790) explained in *The Wealth of Nations* (1776) how the free market operates for the best of all people in capitalism. Capitalism was the system of economics in America throughout its first century.

Christianity was the second great philosophical thinking, or way of life and belief, that led to the American Revolution. Americans' reliance on a Christian God led them to believe it was their God-given right to have a representative government. John Adams, America's second president, wrote that the Revolution "connected, in one indissoluble bond, the principles of civil government with the principles of Christianity." John's cousin Sam Adams wrote that the Declaration "restored the Sovereign to Whom alone men ought to be obedient." Thomas Jefferson wrote in the Declaration of Independence, "…**all men are created equal,** that they are endowed by their Creator with certain unalienable Rights."

Most of the colonial leaders were strong Protestant Christians who believed in a **personal God**. We see this not only in their personal writings, but in the state constitutions with "Supreme Being," "great Creator," and "Preserver of the Universe" written throughout. It is true that Thomas Jefferson and Benjamin Franklin were perhaps **deists**, meaning that they believed in God more as a clock maker who created the world and let it run on its own. However, most colonial leaders believed as George Washington did. He wrote this prayer in 1752, "I humbly beseech Thee to be merciful to me in the free pardon of my sins for the sake of thy dear Son and only Savior Jesus Christ who came to call not the righteous, but sinners to repentance. Thou gavest Thy Son to die for me."

Facts to Know for The Ideas of Revolution

1. Enlightenment: The Enlightenment was an intellectual movement where individuals, primarily in Europe in the 1700s, believed that man could understand the world by using reason.

2. Thomas Hobbes: Englishman Thomas Hobbes (1588-1679) wrote in his book *Leviathan* that man's life, without government, was "solitary, poor, nasty, brutish, and short." Government was created to protect life, and a monarch could have absolute power to do this.

3. John Locke: Englishman John Locke (1632-1704) wrote that government's job was to be limited to protecting life, liberty, and property. With a limited role, people would have maximum liberty.

4. Baron Charles de Montesquieu: French author Montesquieu (1689-1755) wrote that to limit the abuse of power, government should be broken into three branches. Each branch would be responsible for some power, and each would make sure the other branches did not get too much control.

5. Adam Smith: Smith (1723-1790) explained in *The Wealth of Nations* (1776) how the free market operates for the best of all people in capitalism. Capitalism was the system of economics in America throughout its first century.

6. Christianity: Americans' reliance on a Christian God led them to believe it was their God-given right to have a representative government. John Adams, America's second

president, wrote that the Revolution "connected, in one indissoluble bond, the principles of civil government with the principles of Christianity." John's cousin Sam Adams wrote that the Declaration "restored the Sovereign to Whom alone men ought to be obedient." Thomas Jefferson wrote in the Declaration of Independence, "…all men are created equal, that they are endowed by their Creator with certain unalienable Rights."

7. All men are created equal: Thomas Jefferson wrote, "all men are created equal" as part of this founding document. This means that God is the Creator of life, and that all people are born with the same political rights.

8. Personal God: to believe in a personal God means to devote one's life to God, to love God, and to believe that God is personally involved in one's life. Most of the American Founding Fathers viewed God in this manner.

9. Deist: Thomas Jefferson and Benjamin Franklin were perhaps deists, meaning that they believed in God more as a clock maker who created the world and let it run on its own.

10. The Wealth of Nations: Adam Smith (1723-1790) explained in *The Wealth of Nations* (1776) how the free market operates for the best of all people in capitalism.

66. Lexington and Concord: April 19, 1775

The beginning of the American Revolution took place primarily in New England. The first fight of the war was not a traditional battle of two armies, but instead a skirmish, a fight that was not premeditated, between small opposing groups. Though small, the **Lexington and Concord skirmish** had monumental ramifications. The skirmish at Lexington and Concord was fought because the British tried to stop the Americans from preparing for war. In 1774, American leaders at the Continental Congress in Philadelphia petitioned King George III and Parliament to restore their rights. When the king and Parliament refused and continued to hold the people of Boston under **martial law**, the Americans decided to mobilize for war. Colonists established illegal, revolutionary governments, collected taxes to fund militias and even funerals for soldiers, and established **arsenals**, which are warehouses for guns and ammunition. Americans were already well-armed, with each family owning several guns. However, men in villages now trained as soldiers. Town leaders chose and financially supported some soldiers, called **minutemen**, to be prepared to fight within a minute's notice.

General Gage, the commander of the British army in Boston, wanted to surprise the colonists. He ordered Major Pitcairn to march 1,000 soldiers 20 miles to Concord to destroy colonial ammunition and to arrest Samuel Adams and John Hancock. Americans in Boston learned of this plan and spoiled the surprise. On the night of April 18, 1775, a Bostonian set **two lanterns** in the belfry tower of the Old North Church, thus signaling to three riders, Dr. Samuel Prescott, William Dawes and Paul Revere, that the British would go to Concord initially by a sea route. The three riders set off from Boston to Concord, warning the colonists, "**The Regulars are coming!** The Regulars are coming!" The "Regulars" were the professional British soldiers. The three successfully alerted the colonists to arm themselves and meet the British.

On the morning of April 19, 1775, the American Revolution started. About 700 British Regulars met less than 100 volunteer Americans assembled in Lexington, a village along the road to Concord. When the Regulars met the Americans, it was dark. Major Pitcairn ordered the Americans to disperse. They just stood there. Then, inexplicably, a shot rang out and the fighting started. The British killed eight and the Americans scattered. The British continued their march to Concord. In Concord, the British found the weapons and destroyed them. However, the Americans gathered there in far greater numbers and defeated a smaller group of the British at the **Old North Bridge**. This victory energized the colonists.

The British were now twenty miles away from Boston, in the middle of hostile territory. For the rest of the day, the Regulars marched back to the city, drums beating, in formation, along a narrow road. During this march, Americans took aim at the soldiers, firing behind trees, stone walls, and fences, and then running away when any British soldier would chase them. British losses included 73 killed, 174 wounded, and 26 missing in action. American losses were 49 killed, 39 wounded, and 5 missing. Though a small victory, it was seen as a great triumph for the Americans over the strongest empire in the world. The shot that started the war has been called "The shot heard 'round the world."

Facts to Know for Lexington and Concord: April 19, 1775

1. Lexington and Concord skirmish: On April 19, 1775, the American Revolution started with the skirmish at Lexington and Concord.

2. Martial Law: Martial law means military law. The entire population is under the strict rule of the military.

3. General Gage: General Gage was the commander of the British army in Boston.

4. Arsenal: An arsenal is a warehouse for guns and ammunition.

5. Minutemen: Town leaders chose and financially supported some soldiers, called minutemen, to be prepared to fight within a minute's notice.

6. Major Pitcairn: Major Pitcairn marched 1,000 soldiers 20 miles to Concord to destroy colonial ammunition and to arrest Samuel Adams and John Hancock.

7. Two Lanterns: The night of April 18, 1775, a Bostonian set two lanterns in the belfry tower of the Old North Church, thus signaling to three riders, Dr. Samuel Prescott, William Dawes and Paul Revere, that the British would go to Concord initially by a sea route.

8. The Regulars are Coming: The three riders set off from Boston to Concord, warning the colonists, "The Regulars are coming! The Regulars are coming!" The "Regulars" were the professional British soldiers.

9. Old North Bridge: At the skirmish of Lexington and Concord, the Americans gathered at the Old North Bridge and defeated a smaller group of British soldiers.

10. The Shot Heard 'Round the World: The shot heard 'round the world refers to the first shot fired at the skirmish at Lexington and Concord.

67. Siege of Boston

After the skirmish at Lexington and Concord in 1775, American colonists laid **siege** to the city of Boston. British soldiers, led by General Gage, controlled the city, but Americans controlled the countryside. The beginning of the war was at a standstill.

Thousands more Americans rushed to the aid of the Bostonians, setting up camp around the city, and trapping the British soldiers. Inside of Boston, Americans occupied Charlestown Peninsula, building fortifications on Breed's Hill and Bunker Hill. The British attacked, and the Americans fought bravely. Realizing their shortage of bullets and supplies, American Colonel William Prescott ordered his men to conserve their bullets. Reportedly, Israel Putnam said, "Don't one of you fire until you see the white of their eyes." The Americans lost the **Battle of Bunker Hill**, but shocked the British by killing and wounding many. Half of the British were either wounded or killed, and 12% of all British officers killed in the war died at this battle.

After the Battle of Bunker Hill, the American Congress realized that the war against Britain had begun, and made the crucial decision of the war: naming George Washington as **Commander of the Continental Army.** Washington immediately left Philadelphia for Boston, and took command of the **30,000 soldiers** surrounding the city, and made plans to beat the British.

Boston bookseller and now army officer **Henry Knox** suggested to Washington that he order men to march about 300 miles north to capture **Fort Ticonderoga**, then take the cannons from the fort, and drag them back to Boston. In January 1776, Knox arrived with the cannons. Washington positioned the cannons on **Dorchester Heights** overlooking Boston, and fired on the British. Realizing their hopeless position, the British fled by way of their navy.

The beginning of the American Revolution went amazingly well for the Americans. The Americans successfully beat the British at Lexington and Concord, fought extremely well at the Battle of Bunker Hill, and chased the British Army from Boston.

Facts to Know for the Siege of Boston

1. Siege: a military operation in which enemy forces surround a town or building, cutting off essential supplies, with the aim of compelling the surrender of those inside.

2. The Battle of Bunker Hill: During the siege of Boston, British soldiers attacked the Americans, who were fortified on Breed's Hill. The British won, but suffered incredible losses.

3. Commander of the Continental Army: The Continental Congress chose George Washington to lead the army of the United States of America, known as the Continental Army.

4. 30,000 soldiers: At the beginning of the American Revolution, the Continental Army had 30,000 soldiers. At its lowest point, it had under 5,000.

5. Henry Knox: Boston bookseller turned army officer Henry Knox marched his men about 300 miles north to Fort Ticonderoga then dragged 60 tons of military supplies including 59 artillery pieces and dragged them back to Boston.

6. Fort Ticonderoga: Fort Ticonderoga was about 300 miles from Boston, located between New York's Adirondack and Vermont's Green Mountains. It was held by the British, who did not expect and American attack. Three weeks after the skirmish at Lexington and Concord, American leaders Ethan Allen and Benedict Arnold led a band of Vermont's Green Mountain Boys and captured the fort.

7. Dorchester Heights: These hills overlook Boston. Upon these hills, Washington had his men position the artillery pieces Knox brought back from Fort Ticonderoga.

68. The Declaration of Independence

On **July 4, 1776**, delegates at the Continental Congress approved the Declaration of Independence. This document is one of the most important in history and shows the ideals and achievements of the American Founding Fathers. It is a work that does two things: it declares **universal ideals** for all people throughout the world, and it states that the United States of America is independent of Great Britain. **Thomas Jefferson** was the main author of the Declaration of Independence, and **Benjamin Franklin and John Adams** helped him edit and revise it. Jefferson took much of his writing from Englishman **John Locke**. Locke had written that government's job was to be limited to protecting life, liberty, and property. With a limited role, people would have maximum liberty. Jefferson and the Founding Fathers completely agreed with Locke.

In 1859, Abraham Lincoln wrote of the Declaration of Independence:

> All honor to Jefferson-to the man who, in the concrete pressure of a struggle for national independence by a single people, had the coolness, forecast, and capacity to introduce into a merely revolutionary document, an abstract truth, applicable to all men and all times, and so to embalm it there, that to-day, and in all coming days, it shall be a rebuke and a stumbling block to the very harbingers of re-appearing tyranny and oppression.

In the Declaration of Independence, Jefferson built on John Locke's ideas to write the ideals of the new nation, "We hold these truths to be self-evident, that **all men are**

created equal." The notion that all men are created equal involves a number of ideas. The first is that there is one Creator of all men. Jefferson and the Founding Fathers believed in one God who created all things. The second idea in this statement is that the Creator gave all humans political equality. At birth, people were meant to have the same rights. One person was not intended to have more rights than another. In the British system, and in much of the world at the time, certain people in society had more rights than others. In the new United States of America, the ideal was for political equality.

Jefferson continued the Declaration by writing, "that they are endowed by their Creator with certain **unalienable Rights**; that among these are Life, Liberty, and the pursuit of Happiness." These are commonly referred to as "**natural rights**," as described by John Locke. They are natural because man has them through birth. No government gives man these rights. They are his naturally, from God. The right to life means that nobody is allowed to take a human life. Murder is against the law. **Liberty** means the right to political freedoms, such as the right of free speech and free press, and the right of religious freedom. The pursuit of happiness has commonly been understood to mean the right to own **private property**, but it also seems to imply more than this. In most of the world in the 1700s, people were not allowed to own property. Property was the right held only by the ruler, or by the ruling class. In the new country of the U.S.A., the American Founding Fathers firmly believed in every man's right to own land. This right allowed a person independence from the government, and the ability to establish a family and enjoy the fruits of one's labor.

Facts to Know for
The Declaration of Independence

1. July 4, 1776: On July 4, 1776, delegates at the Continental Congress approved the Declaration of Independence.

2. Universal Ideals: Universal ideals are those things that people all over the world strive for. These ideals are not limited to one nation or ethnic group, but have universal (worldwide) appeal.

3. Thomas Jefferson: Thomas Jefferson (1743-1826) was the primary author of the Declaration of Independence.

4. Benjamin Franklin and John Adams: Benjamin Franklin (1706-1790) and John Adams (1735-1826) edited the Declaration of Independence.

5. John Locke: Many ideas Thomas Jefferson wrote about in the Declaration of Independence were inspired by the writings of John Locke (1632-1704).

6. All Men Are Created Equal: Thomas Jefferson wrote this in the Declaration of Independence. It means that God created all individuals with the same rights, and that no government had the right to favor one person over another.

7. Unalienable Rights: Unalienable rights means those rights that cannot be legitimately taken away.

8. Natural Rights: John Locke wrote, and Thomas Jefferson agreed, that natural rights were given to man by God.

Natural rights refer to life, liberty, and private property/pursuit of happiness.

9. Liberty: Liberty means the right to political freedoms, such as the right of free speech and free press, and the right of religious freedom

10. Private Property: Private property is land or materials owned by an individual. In 1776, in every place of the world except the United States of America, only certain individuals were allowed to own private property. John Locke wrote, and Thomas Jefferson affirmed in the Declaration of Independence, that the right to own private property is a natural right.

69. Early Battles and the Winter at Valley Forge

Just a month and a half after the signing of the Declaration of Independence, George Washington and the American Army were crushed at the **Battle of Long Island**. English brothers General Howe and Admiral Howe and over 35,000 British and Hessian (paid fighters from Hesse, Germany) soldiers and sailors nearly destroyed, captured, or scattered all of Washington's army of about 20,000. To the surprise of the British, Washington somehow escaped a seemingly hopeless situation with 3,000 American soldiers. Because of Washington's ability to lead his army away from capture, the British called him "the silver fox."

Demoralized and in a dire situation, the soldiers of the Continental Army were in danger of disbanding and losing the war. Many soldiers had initially signed up to fight for **90 days**, and it would not have been viewed as cowardice had they left. It was then that Washington ordered a daring attack that captured the imaginations of Americans then and today. On Christmas night, December 25, 1776, the Continental Army crossed the **icy Delaware River** and surprised 1,000 Hessian soldiers who had been celebrating Christmas, in part, by drinking large amounts of hard alcohol. The Americans captured the town of **Trenton**, and gained immeasurable amounts of enthusiasm and hope. Within the month, Washington led his soldiers in defeating the British, again, at the **Battle of Princeton** (1777), bravely riding his horse in between the British and American lines, calling out to his men, "Parade with us, my brave fellows…we will have them directly."

Perhaps the American low point of the war was the fall and winter of 1777-1778. The British defeated the Americans at the **Battles of Brandywine and Germantown**, and captured Philadelphia. The one bright spot for the Americans was that they won the **Battle of Saratoga** in the Mohawk Valley, defeating an army of 6,000 soldiers. While the British enjoyed the warmth of Philadelphia and New York City, the Americans spent the winter at **Valley Forge**, Pennsylvania, a cold and inadequately supplied fort. It was here that the American soldiers nearly lost all hope. They were poorly fed, lacked basic winter clothes, and felt abandoned by the American Congress and people.

One thing that kept up the hopes of Americans was the writings of **Thomas Paine**. A recent immigrant to America from England, Paine had failed in business and in two marriages. His second wife paid him to leave her. However, Paine wrote perhaps the most inspiring revolutionary essays in *Common Sense*, and later, *The American Tract*. Paine wrote, "These are the times that try men's souls. The summer soldier and the sunshine patriot will, in this crisis, shrink from the service of his country." American soldiers read from these books during their winter months.

But perhaps the most important factor in turning the tide of war at Valley Forge was the training of American farmers into a hardened, professional army. Foreign officers joined the Americans and trained the farmer volunteers. **German Baron von Steuben, French nobleman Lafayette, Polish Count Pulaski** and others voluntarily trained and fought alongside the Americans. After the winter of Valley Forge, the Continental Army was ready for battle.

Facts to Know for Early Battles and the Winter at Valley Forge

1. Battle of Long Island: George Washington and the Continental Army suffered a devastating defeat at the Battle of Long Island (1776). Out of 20,000 soldiers, Washington escaped with only 3,000.

2. 90 Days: Most American soldiers originally signed up to fight for 90 days.

3. Icy Delaware River: On Christmas night 1776, Washington led his army across the icy Delaware River in a brave attack on the enemy at Trenton.

4. Trenton: After crossing the icy Delaware River, Washington and his army captured the enemy at the Battle of Trenton.

5. Battle of Princeton: At the Battle of Princeton (1777), Washington engaged in hand-to-hand combat to defeat the British.

6. Battles of Brandywine and Germantown: At the Battles of Brandywine and Germantown (1777), the British defeated the Americans.

7. Battle of Saratoga: In 1777, the Americans won the Battle of Saratoga.

8. Valley Forge: During the winter of 1777-1778, Americans stayed at Valley Forge. Conditions were harsh, but Americans also trained to be professional soldiers.

9. Thomas Paine: Thomas Paine, an English immigrant, wrote inspiring revolutionary essays in *Common Sense*, and later, *The American Tract.* American soldiers read these on the battlefields and in their camps.

10. German Baron von Steuben, French nobleman Lafayette, and Polish Count Pulaski: German Baron von Steuben, French nobleman Lafayette, and Polish Count Pulaski and others voluntarily trained and fought alongside the Americans.

70. The French and Southern Phase of the War

After the winter at Valley Forge, British General "Gentleman" **Johnny Burgoyne** moved to invade the Mohawk Valley in New York, but in his entourage were 400 women camp-followers, his mistress, his four-poster bed, fine china, best dress clothes, and other needless people and materials. Burgoyne met a tough and well-trained professional army. American General Horatio Gates had 12,000 militia and 5,000 regulars against Burgoyne's army of 6,000. In two engagements known as the **Battle of Saratoga**, the Americans completely destroyed or captured Burgoyne's army.

After the Americans won the Battle of Saratoga, French King Louis XVI was persuaded by American ambassador Benjamin Franklin that the Americans could win the war. **The French** joined the Americans in war against the British in February 1778, sending 30,000 muskets, 200 cannon, 25,000 uniforms, 1,000,000 pounds of powder (90% of total American powder), the French fleet, and a French army.

While the British defeated the Americans in most of the battles and occupied the major cities of New England and the Middle Colonies, they could not keep control of the countryside. The war was in a stalemate. The British decided they would focus their efforts in the South, where a greater percentage of Americans sided with Great Britain than in the North. In the South, however, Americans caused great harm to the British. **"Swamp Fox" Francis Marion,** Thomas Sumter, and Andrew Pickens led southern militia forces against the British. Nathaniel Greene led his soldiers in defeating the British at the **Battle of Cowpens**, South

Carolina, and badly hurt the British at the Battle of Guilford Courthouse in North Carolina.

French **Commander Rochambeau** devised a trick that eventually led to the end of the war. Washington pretended to march soldiers to attack New York, but actually marched 5,000 soldiers to join with 5,000 French and met with Nathaniel Greene's army, who had outmaneuvered British General **Lord Cornwallis**. While these three armies surrounded Cornwallis at **Yorktown, Virginia**, the French fleet beat the English navy at sea, blocking the British escape. After some fighting, Cornwallis saw that his position was hopeless, and he surrendered on October 19, 1781. Americans captured 8,000 soldiers, 214 artillery pieces, thousands of muskets, and 24 transport ships. Even though the war continued for two more years, there were no other major engagements in North America, and the British lost interest in continuing to fight.

The first country in the modern era had won its independence from a colonial power and the **world's first modern republic** was established. To win the war, **Washington** realized that it was more important to never suffer such a defeat that he or all his men would be captured, and he outmaneuvered the British until France decided to send help. Between 40,000 and 60,000 American patriots gave their lives for their new country.

Facts to Know for The French and Southern Phase of the War

1. Johnny Burgoyne: British General "Gentleman" Johnny Burgoyne led his army and many followers into the Mohawk Valley of New York.

2. Battle of Saratoga: American General Horatio Gates crushed Burgoyne's army and won a stunning and important victory.

3. The French: After the Battle of Saratoga, French King Louis XVI decided to support the Americans with massive amounts of military aid, weapons, ammunition, soldiers, and his navy.

4. Swamp Fox Francis Marion: Marion, and others, defeated the British in their many efforts to subdue the South.

5. Battle of Cowpens: American Nathaniel Greene defeated the British at this battle in South Carolina.

6. French Commander Rochambeau: He devised a trick that eventually led to the end of the war. Washington faked maneuvering men to attack New York City, but really led his men to join others at Yorktown to defeat the British.

7. Lord Cornwallis: This British General was perhaps the most respected British general in the war.

8. Battle of Yorktown: General George Washington defeated General Cornwallis in what would become the last battle of the American Revolution on October 19, 1781.

9. World's First Modern Republic: The United States of America became the world's first modern republic.

10. George Washington: Washington realized that it was wise to never allow his army to be captured. He fought the war until he had an advantage, namely, the French joining the war. Then, when he saw the opportunity, he acted with decisiveness and defeated the British.

71. The Trans-Mississippi West, 1865-90

Railroads spurred the westward expansion in the late nineteenth century. In 1869 the "**Golden Spike**" was driven that completed the Union Pacific Railroad from Omaha, Nebraska, to Sacramento, California. Ultimately, the nineteenth century United States boasted five trans-continentals, and Canadians built one. Privately funded railroads like James J. Hill's **Great Northern** operated much more efficiently than those that relied on government subsidies and land grants. Wood- and coal-generated steam trans-continental railroads carried settlers, troops, businessmen, and tons of supplies Westward, while shipping cattle, agricultural produce, and mining ore Eastward.

The **California Gold Rush of 1849** was followed by subsequent mining rushes across the American and Canadian West, ending finally in Alaska in 1898. The first miners to rush into California were known as '**49ers**. Wild mining camps were initially tamed by self-governing miners' associations and, ultimately, territorial governments. Mining practices evolved rapidly from the independent miner **panning for gold** to hydraulic mining by salaried workers supervised by trained mining engineers. Where gold became scarce, miners found silver, copper ore, coal, and more plentiful minerals.

America's westward expansion led to warfare and defeat of native Indian people. The **final Indian wars** were fought on the Great Plains, where natives armed with repeating rifles and mounted on horseback fiercely fought the U.S. Army. Four major wars took place during and after the U.S. Civil War in the modern-day states of Colorado, Wyoming, Texas, Oklahoma, and Montana. With great difficulty, the U.S. Army defeated Cheyenne, Arapaho, Comanche, Kiowa, Lakota (Sioux), Apache and other tribal warriors.

In 1876-77, despite the Lakota victory over General George Armstrong Custer at the **Battle of the Little Bighorn** and **Nez Perce Chief Joseph**'s brave resistance, the wars ended. Those Indians who survived were forced to give up their nomadic lifestyle and live on reservation.

A myth is a story that has great meaning to a people. Great myths are based on a core of truth. **The Myth of the West** is the story of courageous American people moving westward across the continent. As they advanced, Americans met and tamed the wilderness and defeated fierce adversaries. In the mythic view, they prevailed because progress and civilization were inevitable. But the historic view shows that Indians, Mexicans, and others paid a high price for westward expansion. The Myth of the West became the basis for "Westerns" in literature, movies, and television. Daniel Boone, Jim Beckwourth, "Calamity Jane" Canary, and Buffalo Bill Cody became mythic heroes.

Facts to Know for
The Trans-Mississippi West, 1865-90

1. The Golden Spike: In 1869, this was the last spike that was driven that completed the Union Pacific Railroad from Omaha, Nebraska, to Sacramento, California.

2. Great Northern: Entrepreneur James J. Hill built a transcontinental railroad with private funds.

3. California Gold Rush of 1849: Over 100,000 men from around the world rushed into California seeking gold.

4. '49ers: Men who rushed in seeking gold in California in 1849 were called "the "49ers."

5. Panning for Gold: Individuals trying to get gold used a pan to sift the gold from the sand and rocks.

6. Final Indian Wars: The last Indian wars were fought on the Great Plains after the Civil War.

7. Battle of Little Bighorn: The Lakota annihilated General George Armstrong Custer and his men at this battle.

8. Nez Perce Chief Joseph: Chief Joseph and the Nez Perce fought bravely against the American Army before surrendering.

9. The Myth of the West: This myth is the idea that the American Westward expansion was only a story of progress and civilization and ignored the sufferings of Native Americans and Mexicans.

72. America Enters the World Stage and World War I, 1898-1917

Having conquered the West, purchased Alaska, and annexed Midway Island in the 1860s and 70s, the U.S. government continued territorial expansion in the Pacific in the 1890s. Americans were motivated by economics, religion, scientific curiosity, and military strategy. Sugar cane and pineapple investor **Samuel Dole** convinced President Benjamin Harrison to send U.S. sailors to help oust Hawaiian Queen Liliuokalani in 1893. In 1898, during the Spanish-American War, **President William McKinley** annexed Hawaii and appointed Dole territorial governor. McKinley also oversaw the annexation of the Pacific islands of **Wake and Samoa** in 1899 and 1900. Like North American Indians, Pacific Island natives were forced to live under the governance of the United States.

Spain's empire was in decline in the late 1800s and the United States had economic, religious, and strategic motives to take Spain's place. In 1898, the American ship *U.S.S. Maine* was blown up in Spanish Cuba and America blamed Spain. Under President McKinley, U.S. armed forces were victorious in the **Spanish-American War** (1898) in Cuba and the Philippines. After a bloody civil war with former Philippine allies, Americans annexed the Philippines alongside Spanish Guam, and Puerto Rico. The Philippines eventually gained independence, but Guam and Puerto Rico remain American territories with political representation. McKinley also announced an **"Open Door"** policy to access Chinese trade.

Progressives favored big government at home and expansion abroad. While motivated to defeat oppressors and spread Christianity and republicanism, Progressives also had self-serving economic and military goals.

President Theodore Roosevelt urged Americans to "walk softly and carry a big stick"! He ordered U.S. Marines into the Dominican Republic and Panama, ensuring completion of the **Panama Canal** connecting the Pacific and Caribbean. President Woodrow Wilson followed suit, invading Mexico in 1914 in pursuit of the famous Mexican leader Pancho Villa and purchasing the Caribbean Virgin Islands from Denmark in 1916. Wilson also stationed U.S. Marines in Haiti and Nicaragua, starting a series of **"Banana Wars"** sarcastically named for U.S. banana growers.

Although Progressives intervened in Latin America and the Pacific Islands, they initially followed the old Monroe Doctrine promise to stay out of European affairs. This was called **"isolationism."** However, 1917 saw a temporary end to isolationism when America entered **World War I** (WWI) allied with Britain, France, and Russia against Germany and its allies. World War I marked the beginning of **"total war,"** with airplanes, machine guns, tanks, submarines, poison gas, and civilian casualties. American forces tipped the scales and won victory in what President Woodrow Wilson mistakenly called the **"war to end all wars."** In fact, the revengeful **Treaty of Versailles** ending WWI set the stage for World War II.

Facts to Know for America Enters the World Stage and World War I, 1898-1918

1. Samuel Dole: He was a sugar cane and pineapple investor who became Hawaii's first territorial governor.

2. President William McKinley: This President led the United States in winning the Spanish American war (1898) and taking the following territories: Cuba, Puerto Rico, the Phillipines, Wake, Samoa, Guam.

3. Wake and Samoa: The United States of America annexed these islands in 1899 and 1900.

4. U.S.S. Maine: In 1898, the American ship U.S.S. Maine was blown up in Spanish Cuba and America blamed Spain. This resulted in the Spanish American War (1898).

5. Open Door Policy: President McKinley forced China to have an advantageous trading policy with the United States of America.

6. Progressives: These favored big government at home and expansion abroad.

7. President Theodore Roosevelt: He ordered U.S. Marines into the Dominican Republic and Panama, ensuring completion of the Panama Canal connecting the Pacific and Caribbean.

8. Banana Wars: The United States aided allies and agricultural companies in a series of wars in Latin America, and "Banana Wars" was the name sarcastically given to these wars.

9. Isolationism: This was the American policy before World War I to stay out of the affairs of Europe.

10. World War I: Lasting from 1914-1918, one side (the Triple Alliance) included Germany, Austria-Hungary, and Italy, and also the Ottoman Empire, and the other (the Triple Entente) included Great Britain, France, Russia until 1918, and the United States of America from 1917.

11. Total War: World War I marked the beginning of "total war," with airplanes, machine guns, tanks, submarines, poison gas, and civilian casualties.

12. War to End All Wars: Many, including Woodrow Wilson, called World War I this.

13. Versailles Treaty: This treaty ended World War I and placed great blame on Germany.

73. The "Roaring 20s"

Following World War I, Americans reversed course by electing Republican Senator Warren G. Harding President with 61% of the vote. Harding pledged a "**return to normalcy**" away from Progressivism with freer markets and isolationism. Harding died in office and Vice **President Calvin Coolidge** successfully carried on from 1923-1928. Announcing "the business of America is business," Coolidge cut taxes, reduced business regulations and government expenses, and balanced the federal budget. In foreign affairs he kept America out of the **League of Nations**, imposed tariffs on foreign competitors, reduced the U.S. military, and refused diplomatic recognition to communist Soviet Union. Meanwhile, the economy and stock market soared.

The 1920s brought great changes to the lives of common Americans. More middle-class families owned automobiles, and the newly invented radio brought music, news, and sports into peoples' homes. "**Movie stars**" like Mary Pickford and Charlie Chaplin arose and thousands watched and tuned into coach Knute Rockne's Notre Dame football squad and the annual Army vs Navy football game. In professional sports, Americans idolized black boxer **Joe Lewis** and the New York Yankee baseball slugger Babe Ruth. However, the greatest American hero of all was aviator **Charles Lindbergh**. "Lucky Lindy" flew his airplane--dubbed "The Spirit of St. Louis"--non-stop from New York City to Paris in May of 1927.

1920s women saw transformation in their political, economic, and cultural lifestyles. First-time female voters helped elect Presidents Harding, Coolidge, and Hoover to office. The Industrial Revolution reduced housework thanks to appliances, store-bought clothes, canned goods, and bakeries, and now 10% of the workforce outside the home were women. Open displays of sexuality characterized what was called a "revolution in manners and morals." Women wore cosmetics, cut their hair in short, fashionable "bobs," and sported flesh-colored stockings with thin, sleeveless dresses with hemlines 9" above the ground. Some modern women were called "**Flappers**," and one writer noted, "With hair bobbed, face painted, and cigarette in hand, she airily waved goodbye to yesterday's standards."

For every action there is a reaction, and the booming 1920s American economy was followed by a terrible stock market "crash" and the **Great Depression**. The crash and Depression were caused by too much credit (buying without cash at hand), overproduction (too many goods and fewer buyers), tariffs, agricultural downturn, and world-wide depression, especially in Europe. **President Herbert Hoover** (1929-1933) was a Progressive Republican whose economic regulations, federal loans, and public construction projects (like Hoover Dam) foreshadowed those of Franklin Roosevelt. But Hoover was overwhelmed as unemployment rose to 25% and national income was cut in half. In 1932, the Democrats returned to power.

Facts to Know for The "Roaring 20s"

1. Return to Normalcy: President Warren G. Harding pledged a "return to normalcy" away from Progressivism with freer markets and isolationism and was reelected with 61% of the popular vote in 1920.

2. President Calvin Coolidge: He took over after the death of President Harding, and served from 1923-1929. He famously said, "The business of America is business."

3. League of Nations: The Treaty of Versailles established a League of Nations. This was something similar to the United Nations. The United States of America never joined.

4. Movie Stars: The 1920s saw Americans very excited for the first time about movie stars, such as Mary Pickford and Charlie Chaplin.

5. Joe Lewis: He was a very successful and famous boxer in the 1920s.

6. Charles Lindbergh: Nicknamed "Lucky Lindy," he flew his airplane--dubbed "The Spirit of St. Louis"--non-stop from New York City to Paris in May of 1927.

7. 1920s Women: They saw transformation in their political, economic, and cultural lifestyles.

8. Flappers: Some women were called this. They had hair bobbed, face painted, and smoked cigarettes.

9. The Great Depression: This great economic downturn lasted from 1929-1939.

10. President Herbert Hoover (1929-1933): He was a Progressive Republican whose economic regulations, federal loans, and public construction projects (like Hoover Dam) foreshadowed those of Franklin Roosevelt.

74. World War II, 1941-45

In **World War II**, the United States allied with Britain, France, the Soviet Union, and China to fight fascist "Axis" powers Germany, Italy, and Japan. American forces— which included black, Indian, and female enlistees and draftees—joined Allies in attacking Nazi Germany and Italy from north Africa and western France while Soviets fought Germany on the "Russian Front." As Germany weakened, the United States shifted focus to the Pacific war against Japan. "**VE Day**"—Victory in Europe Day—came at last on May 8, 1945 while Japan surrendered on September 2, 1945, "**VJ Day.**" 400,000 Americans lost their lives in World War II and the United States emerged as a major world power.

While World War II raged abroad, the U.S. home front changed dramatically. Women stepped up to war production jobs, making up **57%** of the workforce. Americans purchased government "war bonds" to help fund the war, planted "victory gardens" to conserve food, collected scrap metal and rubber, and accepted hardships like stringent rationing of gasoline, meat, shoes, and sugar. The federal government workforce grew 400% and so did its power to control wages, prices, rents, and production schedules. The national debt and taxes soared. Americans learned that a government powerful enough to win a world war was also powerful enough to suspend constitutional liberties for **Japanese Americans**. Yet this remarkable war mobilization led to victory.

Adolph Hitler, leader of Nazi Germany, was a racist who despised Jews, Slavs, blacks, and other minorities. Hitler proposed a "**Final Solution**" for "Mongrel Races" through genocide—the intentional act of destroying a people in whole or part. American troops learned to their horror what a madman Hitler was. In German "concentration camps" they found incinerators, gas chambers, and thousands of dead bodies. The Nazis had murdered 10,000,000 innocent civilians, including 6,000,000 Jews. U.S. General Dwight Eisenhower stated that he had "never at any time experienced an equal sense of shock." Soon after the war, the United Nations created the state of **Israel** as a homeland for Jews who survived this "Holocaust."

Although 400,000 American soldiers died in World War II, the toll could have been much higher if America had invaded mainland Japan. The Japanese ferociously opposed U.S. Marine Corps, Army, and Navy forces advancing across the Pacific islands and often chose suicide over surrender. By the summer of 1945, President Harry S. Truman decided to avoid further American deaths by deploying the newly invented **Atom Bomb**—the most powerful weapon in the history of warfare. On August 6 and 9, Americans dropped two bombs on the Japanese cities of Hiroshima and Nagasaki. Over 200,000 civilians died. Japan soon surrendered and World War II ended. The Atom Bomb proved so horrific that no nation has dared use it since.

Facts to Know for World War II, 1941-45

1. World War II: The United States allied with Britain, France, the Soviet Union, and China (the Allies) to fight fascist "Axis" powers Germany, Italy, and Japan in World War II, 1941-1945.

2. VE Day: This was Victory in Europe Day. It came at last on May 8, 1945.

3. VJ Day: This was Victory in Japan Day. It came on September 2, 1945, VJ Day.

4. 57%: This was the percentage of the American workforce during World War II that was made up of women.

5. Japanese Americans: During World War II, Americans forced Japanese Americans off+ their land to concentration camps located in the interior of the county.

6. Adolph Hitler: He was leader of Nazi Germany, was a racist who despised Jews, Slavs, blacks, and other minorities, and in many ways, he started World War II.

7. Final Solution: This was the plan to murder all of the Jews in Europe the Nazis wanted to fulfill.

8. Holocaust: This is the era in which the Nazis murdered up to 6,000,000 Jews.

9. Israel United Nations created the state of Israel as a homeland for Jews who survived this "Holocaust."

10. Atom Bomb: President Truman decided to drop two atom bombs on Japan to avoid American deaths that would have resulted in invading Japan.

75. The 1960s

Massachusetts Senator **John F. Kennedy** served less than three years as President before an assassin killed him. A beloved figure during his short time in office, Kennedy established the **Peace Corps** to aid developing nations and had mixed results in foreign policy. He cut taxes to stimulate the economy and founded America's **Apollo** outer space program. Although Cuba had fallen to the communists in 1959, the staunchly anti-communist Kennedy approved the failed **Bay of Pigs** invasion. He later stood up to Cuba's Soviet allies with a naval blockade in what is now called the **Cuban Missile Crisis**. Kennedy sent 16,000 American troops to oppose communists in **Vietnam**.

Following the assassination of President John F. Kennedy, Vice President **Lyndon B. Johnson** ("LBJ") served as President from 1963-68. A Texan and staunch Democrat, Johnson modeled his policies after his hero Franklin D. Roosevelt's New Deal. LBJ pledged to wage a "war on poverty" and create a "**Great Society**." At his urging, Democrats in Congress increased welfare payments and started a food stamp program. They created federally subsidized day care centers and a Job Corps to provide work training young Americans. Senior citizens received federal "**Medicare**" health insurance. Like the New Deal, the Great Society welfare state was funded through deficit spending and, despite some successes, failed to live up to Democrats' high expectations.

During the 1960s, many young American protestors rejected the lifestyle and politics of the older generation. The major catalyst for their protests was civil rights (including women's rights) and opposition to the Vietnam

War. The "**New Left**" was a name for violent campus radicals and Marxists who sought to replace capitalism with socialism. A more numerous and less political group of protestors were called "**hippies**." They opposed authority by "dropping out" of the economic and educational system, growing long hair, wearing frontier-style clothing and beads and moccasins, using mind-altering drugs, and living in group houses and communes that practiced "free love" (non-marital sex). Both the New Left and the hippies influenced American culture.

Americans fought the **Vietnam War** from 1962-73 with the goal of stopping communist **Ho Chi Minh**'s North Vietnamese army from conquering anti-communist South Vietnam. President John F. Kennedy sent 16,000 U.S. troops in 1963, but it was President Lyndon B. Johnson who greatly escalated the conflict, sending 543,000 troops and spending $100 billion dollars. Because Johnson feared Soviet and Chinese intervention, he refused to invade North Vietnam. The war became a stalemate and created fierce opposition on the home front. Republican **President Richard M. Nixon** began to withdraw U. S. troops in 1969. In 1973 the United States of America and South Vietnam reached a peace treaty with North Vietnam. By **1975** the communist North Vietnamese had conquered the south. 57,000 American soldiers died in the Vietnam War.

Facts to Know for the 1960s

1. President John F. Kennedy: He served from 1961-1963, started the Apollo Space Program, the Peace Corps, sent 15,000 troops to Vietnam, cut taxes, approved the Bay of Pigs invasion, and blockaded Cuba in the Cuban Missile Crisis.

2. Peace Corps: This governmental program places American volunteers in developing countries to assist needy people.

3. Bay of Pigs Invasion: After Communist Fidel Castro overthrew Cuban leader Bautista, Kennedy supported Cuban fighters in their attempt to overthrow Castro. It failed.

4. Cuban Missile Crisis: The Soviet Union attempted to place nuclear missiles in Cuba, but Kennedy succeeded in making them withdraw.

5. Vietnam: North Vietnamese Communists fought for control of all Vietnam after World War II and won the war in 1975.

6. President Lyndon B. Johnson: Johnson served from 1963-1969, started a massive welfare reform called the "Great Society," started the Job Corps and Medicare, and sent over 500,000 U.S. soldiers to fight the Communists in Vietnam.

7. Medicare: This is health insurance for all senior citizens that Johnson started.

8. The New Left: This was a name for violent campus radicals and Marxists who sought to replace capitalism with socialism.

9. Hippies: They opposed authority by "dropping out" of the economic and educational system, growing long hair, wearing frontier-style clothing and beads and moccasins, using mind-altering drugs, and living in group houses and communes that practiced "free love" (non-marital sex).

10. Vietnam War: From 1962-1973, the United States of America supported South Vietnam as they fought Communist North Vietnam. The war ended in a peace treaty in 1973 for the USA. Two years later, Communist North Vietnam conquered South Vietnam.

11. Ho Chi Minh: He was the leader of Communist North Vietnam.

12. President Richard M. Nixon: He began to withdraw U. S. troops in 1969. In 1973 the United States of America and South Vietnam reached a peace treaty with North Vietnam.

13. 1975: In this year, Communist North Vietnam conquered South Vietnam.

Made in the USA
Columbia, SC
19 November 2024

47054395R00141